麦格希 中英双语阅读文库

校园幽默故事

在快乐中成长

第2辑

【美】 麦瑟尔德 (Ken Methold) ●主编

张琳琳●译

麦格希中英双语阅读文库编委会●编

全国百佳图书出版单位
吉林出版集团股份有限公司

图书在版编目（CIP）数据

　　校园幽默故事. 第2辑, 在快乐中成长 / (美) 麦瑟尔德 (Ken Methold) 主编 ; 张琳琳译 ; 麦格希中英双语阅读文库编委会编. -- 2版. -- 长春 : 吉林出版集团股份有限公司, 2018.3（2022.1重印）
　　（麦格希中英双语阅读文库）
　　ISBN 978-7-5581-4739-5

　　Ⅰ.①校… Ⅱ.①麦… ②张… ③麦… Ⅲ.①英语—汉语—对照读物②故事—作品集—美国—现代 Ⅳ.①H319.4：I

中国版本图书馆CIP数据核字(2018)第046446号

校园幽默故事　第2辑　在快乐中成长

编：麦格希中英双语阅读文库编委会
插　　画：齐　航　李延霞
责任编辑：沈丽娟
封面设计：冯冯翼
开　　本：660mm × 960mm　1/16
字　　数：237千字
印　　张：10.5
版　　次：2018年3月第2版
印　　次：2022年1月第2次印刷

出　　版：吉林出版集团股份有限公司
发　　行：吉林出版集团外语教育有限公司
地　　址：长春市福祉大路5788号龙腾国际大厦B座7层
电　　话：总编办：0431-81629929
　　　　　发行部：0431-81629927　0431-81629921(Fax)
印　　刷：北京一鑫印务有限责任公司

ISBN 978-7-5581-4739-5　定价：38.00元

前 言

英国思想家培根说过：阅读使人深刻。阅读的真正目的是获取信息，开拓视野和陶冶情操。从语言学习的角度来说，学习语言若没有大量阅读就如隔靴搔痒，因为阅读中的语言是最丰富、最灵活、最具表现力、最符合生活情景的，同时读物中的情节、故事引人入胜，进而能充分调动读者的阅读兴趣，培养读者的文学修养，至此，语言的学习水到渠成。

"麦格希中英双语阅读文库"在世界范围内选材，涉及科普、社会文化、文学名著、传奇故事、成长励志等多个系列，充分满足英语学习者课外阅读之所需，在阅读中学习英语、提高能力。

◎难度适中

本套图书充分照顾读者的英语学习阶段和水平，从读者的阅读兴趣出发，以难易适中的英语语言为立足点，选材精心、编排合理。

◎精品荟萃

本套图书注重经典阅读与实用阅读并举。既包含国内外脍炙人口、耳熟能详的美文，又包含科普、人文、故事、励志类等多学科的精彩文章。

◎功能实用

本套图书充分体现了双语阅读的功能和优势，充分考虑到读者课外阅读的方便，超出核心词表的词汇均出现在使其意义明显的语境之中，并标注释义。

鉴于编者水平有限，凡不周之处，谬误之处，皆欢迎批评教正。

我们真心地希望本套图书承载的文化知识和英语阅读的策略对提高读者的英语著作欣赏水平和英语运用能力有所裨益。

丛书编委会

Contents

1

Kids' Talk

Have you ever listened to young children talking in the *playground*? They are always *boasting*. They say things like, "My Dad's car is bigger than your Dad's," and "My Mom is *smarter* than yours." They *particularly* like to boast about their families.

There were three little boys, Harry, Ted and Gavin, who were

孩子的谈话

你曾经听过孩子们在操场上的谈话吗?他们都很会吹牛。通常这样说"我爸爸的车比你爸爸的大。""我妈妈比你妈妈聪明。"他们尤其喜欢吹嘘家人。

有三个小男孩,哈里、泰德和加文,就很爱吹牛。加文是最能吹嘘

---

playground *n.* 操场;运动场
smart *adj.* 聪明的;精明的

boast *v.* 自吹自擂;自夸
particularly *adv.* 特别地

always boasting. Gavin was the *worst*. Everything about his family was always the best or the biggest or the most expensive. Whatever the others said, he could always go one better.

One day when they were walking to school, Harry said, "My father takes a bath twice a week."

Ted spoke next. "That's nothing," he said. "Taking a bath twice a week is dirty. My father takes a bath every day, sometimes twice a day."

Ted looked at Gavin. Now it was his turn. But what could he say?

"This time," Ted thought, "I'm going to win."

Gavin didn't know what to say. He couldn't say that his father took a bath three times a day. That was *silly*.

的，他家里的每样东西都是最好的、最大的、最贵的。无论别人怎么说，他都能胜一筹。

一天，在上学的路上，哈里说："我爸爸一周洗两次澡。"

泰德接着说："那没有什么，一周就洗两次澡多脏啊！我爸爸每天都洗，有时一天两次。"

泰德看着加文，现在轮到加文了，他会怎么说呢？

"这次我要赢了。"泰德想。

---

worst *adj.* 最差的   silly *adj.* 愚蠢的

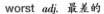

He walked on in *silence*.

Ted smiled at Harry, and Harry smiled back. They were sure that for once they had *beaten* Gavin.

They reached the school gates. Still Gavin said nothing.

They went into class. Morning break, lunchtime, and afternoon *break* all passed. Still Gavin said nothing.

"We've won," Ted said to Harry, but he spoke too soon. On the way home, Gavin said, "My Dad's so clean that he doesn't have to bathe at all."

加文不知道该怎样说，他总不能说他爸爸一天洗三次澡，那样太愚蠢。

他一声不吭地走着。

泰德冲哈里笑笑，哈里也冲泰德笑笑。他们确定这一次打败了加文。

到了校门口，加文还是一声不吭。

他们走进教室，早间休息、午餐时间、下午休息都过去了，加文还是没说什么。

"我们赢了。"泰德对哈里说。可他说得太早了，在放学路上，加文说："我爸爸总那么干净，根本不用洗澡。"

---

silence *n.* 寂静；无声   beat *v.* 击败；战胜

break *n.* 休息

The Monster

Once upon a time there was a *monster*. He was very *ugly* and had no friends. No one wanted to talk to him. Even other monsters thought he was ugly.

He lived alone and was very unhappy because he was so lonely.

"I wish I had a friend," he said to himself every day. "One friend

---

怪物

从前有一只怪物，长得非常丑，也没有朋友。没人想跟他说话，甚至其他怪物也认为他很丑。

他一个人住，非常不开心，因为他是那么孤独。

"我希望有一个朋友，"每天他都自言自语地说："有一个朋友就够了，这样可以跟人说说话。"

---

monster *n.* 怪兽   ugly *adj.* 丑陋的

would be enough. Someone to talk to."

He wrote a letter to a *magazine*. The magazine gave people *advice*.

"Dear *Editor*," he wrote. "I am an ugly monster. How can I find a friend?"

"Dear Monster," the Editor replied. "Advertise for a friend in this magazine."

The monster wrote an *advertisement*.

"Monster wants friend, male or female. I have two heads, four arms, six legs and three tails. I have one blue eye, one green eye and one brown eye. Smoke comes out of my noses. But I am really a kind monster and will be a good friend to someone. If you would like to meet me, please stand outside Blake's Store at 6 in the afternoon on Friday, May 22nd. Write to me at Box 45, Everybody's Magazine."

他给一家杂志社写了一封信，这家杂志常给人们提供一些建议。

"亲爱的编辑，"他写道："我是一只丑陋的怪物，怎样才能找到一个朋友呢？"

"亲爱的怪物，"编辑回信中写道："你可以在这本杂志上登广告找朋友。"

怪物登了一则广告："怪物想交友，男女不限。我有两个头，四只胳膊，六条腿，三条尾巴。我有一只蓝眼睛，一只绿眼睛和一只棕色的眼睛，鼻子会冒烟。但我是一只善良的怪物，而且会成为您的朋友。如果您想见我，请在5月22日星期五晚上六点在布雷克商店外站着。您也可以写

---

magazine *n.* 杂志　　　　　　　　advice *n.* 建议
editor *n.* 编辑　　　　　　　　　advertisement *n.* 广告

A few days later he went to the magazine.

"Do you have any letters for Box 45?" he asked.

The *clerk* looked in Box 45.

"Yes, there is one," she said, and gave it to him.

The monster opened the letter, and read, "Dear Monster, I think a person's *character* is more important than his *appearance*. I will wait outside Blake's Store on Friday. Please carry a flower so that I will *recognize* you. Yours sincerely, Miss Alice Thwaite."

信给我，请寄到《大众杂志》四十五号邮箱。"

几天后他来到杂志社。

"有没有四十五邮箱号的信？"他问。

职员看了看四十五邮箱号。

"是的，有一封。"说完把信递给了他。

怪物打开信念道："亲爱的怪物，我认为一个人的品德要比外表更重要。星期五我会在布雷克商店外等您。请您手里拿一朵花，以便能认出您。您忠诚的，艾丽斯·泰特小姐。"

clerk *n.* 职员

appearance *n.* 外表；外貌

character *n.* 性格

recognize *v.* 认出

3

Directions

A man was trying to find the *village* of Chirton. He could not find any *signs* for it so he decided to drive up to a farmhouse and ask a farmer for *directions*.

He soon came to the *entrance* to a farm. Above the gate there was a sign: Please close the gate.

方向

一个人想去车顿村庄，但他找不到去村庄的任何路标，于是决定开车到一家农舍问路。

他很快来到了农场的入口处，门上有一块提示板，写着"请把门关好"。

village *n.* 村庄
direction *n.* 方向

sign *n.* 标牌
entrance *n.* 入口

The man knew this meant there were cows in the fields, so he was very *careful* to close the gate after him.

Before long he came to another gate. This too, had a sign: Please close the gate. Once again he got out of his car, opened the gate, got back in his car, drove through, stopped his car, got out, closed the gate, got back in his car and drove on.

It wasn't long before he came to a third gate. This too, had a sign: Please close the gate. Again the man got out of his car, opened the gate, got back in his car, drove through, stopped his car, got out, closed the gate, got back in his car and drove on.

He did this five times before he *reached* the farmhouse. *Fortunately*, the farmer was standing at the door.

这人知道这话意味着田地里有牛，因此他小心地把门关好。

很快他来到了另一扇门前，这扇门上也写着"请把门关好"。于是他又一次走下车、打开门、回到车里、开过去、停下来、走下车、关好门、回到车上，继续向前开。

不久，他又来到了第三扇门前，这扇门上同样写着"请把门关好"。于是他又一次走下车、打开门、回到车里、开过去、停下来、走下车、关好门、回到车上，继续向前开。

他到达农舍时，足足重复了五次这样的动作。幸运的是，有一个农民站在门前。

---

careful *adj.* 小心翼翼的   reach *v.* 到达
fortunately *adv.* 幸运的

"What can I do for you?" he asked the man.

"I'm looking for Chirton. Do you know where it is?"

"Sorry," the farmer said. "I've only been here a few weeks. I don't know the *area*."

The man thanked him, and drove back to the road. On the way he had to open and close five gates.

When he reached the road he looked back at the farm. He could see the farmer *waving* to him. "Ah!" he thought, "he's remembered where Chirton is."

He turned around, stopped his car, got out, opened the gate, got back in the car, drove through, stopped the car, got out, closed the gate, got back in the car and drove off. He had to do this five more

---

"有什么需要帮忙的吗？"农民问。

"我想找车顿村庄，您知道它在哪吗？"

"很抱歉，"那个农民说："我刚到这没几周，我不知道那个地方。"

这个人谢过农民，又沿着原路开了回去。在回去的路上他不得不又开关了五次门。

当他到公路上时，又回头望了望农场。他看见农民正在向他挥手。"啊，"心想，"他一定记起车顿在哪呢！"

他转过身，停下车，走出来，打开门，回到车里，开过去，停下来，

---

area *n.* 地区　　　　　　　　　　　　wave *v.* 挥手示意

times before he reached the farm.

"Have you remembered where Chirton is?" he asked the farmer.

"No," the farmer replied, "but I asked my wife. She doesn't know *either*."

走下车，关好门，回到车上，继续向前开。到达农舍前，这些动作又反复了五次。

"您记起车顿在哪了吗？"这个人问农民。

"没有，"那个农民回答说："但我问了我妻子，她也不知道。"

---

either *adv.* 也（不）

Not Such a Simple Question

Alan Robinson was a handsome young man with good *manners*.

One morning he was walking along a street on his way to an *appointment*. He did not want to be late. He had forgotten to put on his watch so he went up to a man who was waiting for a taxi.

一个并不简单的问题

艾伦·罗宾逊是一个英俊潇洒、彬彬有礼的年轻人。

一天早上，他独自上街去赴约。他不想迟到，可他却忘了戴手表，于是他向路边等出租车的人打听。

---

handsome *adj.* 英俊的
appointment *n.* 约会

manners *n.* 礼貌

"Excuse me sir," he said, very *politely*, "but could you tell me the time?"

The man who was very well-dressed and looked quite rich, said nothing. He did not even look at Alan.

Alan spoke to him again. "Excuse me sir," he said, "but could you please tell me what time it is?"

This time the man looked at him, but he did not speak and looked quickly away.

Alan thought to himself: Well, he's not *deaf*. He must be just rude.

"Why won't you tell me the time, sir?" he *demanded*.

The man turned towards him and said, "Try to understand me.

"打扰一下，先生，"他很有礼貌地问，"能告诉我现在几点了吗？"

那个人穿着非常讲究，看起来也很有钱，却一句话也没有说，甚至连看都没看他一眼。

艾伦又对那个人说："对不起，先生，请问您现在几点了？"

这次，那个人看了看艾伦，没说话，把头转向了一边。

艾伦暗自想道："嗯，他不是聋子，他一定很没有礼貌。"

"先生，您为什么不告诉我时间呢？"他问。

那个人转过头对艾伦说："你应该理解我。我正站在路边等出租车，

---

politely *adv.* 客气地

demand *v.* 要求

deaf *adj.* 聋的

12

I am standing here waiting for a taxi. You come up to me and ask me for the time. If I tell it to you, you will thank me. I will say, 'That's all right.' You may then say, 'It's a beautiful day,' to which I may reply, 'Yes, I like these sunny winter days.' Before we know what is happening, we have a friendly conversation. You are a *pleasant*, polite young man and so when my taxi comes, I offer you a ride. You *accept*. We talk. I like you. You like me. I invite you to my home. You meet my daughter. She is a very pretty girl. You are a good-looking man. You like each other. Soon you fall in love. You want to marry. Now do you understand my problem?"

你走过来问我时间。如果我告诉你时间，你就会感谢我。而我应该说'没关系'，然后你也许又会说'多么好的一天啊！'，接着我应该说'是的，我喜欢这样晴朗的冬日'。在我们还没弄清发生了什么事之前，我们已经进行了一次非常友好的谈话。你是一个讨人喜欢、彬彬有礼的年轻人，所以当我的出租车来时，我提出让你一起坐车，你接受了。我们又一起谈话。我喜欢你，你也喜欢我，于是我要请你到我家。在我家你会看见我女儿，她是一个非常漂亮的女孩，你是一个潇洒的年轻人，你们会彼此喜欢，很快会相爱，又会想结婚。现在你理解我的问题了吧？"

pleasant *adj.* 令人愉快的　　　　　　　　　　　　accept *v.* 接受

Alan shook his hand. "No sir, I'm sorry, I don't. Everything you have said seems very *natural* to me."

"Exactly," the man said, "and I do not want my daughter to marry a man who is too poor to buy a watch. Good morning to you."

And with these words he *hurried* away.

艾伦摇摇头说道："不，先生，我很抱歉，我还是不理解。您所说的每件事对我来说再自然不过了。"

"的确如此，"那个人说："我不想我的女儿嫁给一个连表都买不起的人。早上好。"

说完这些话他就匆匆走开了。

---

natural *adj.* 平常的   hurry *v.* 赶紧；急忙

Right Way — Wrong Way

This is a very sad story. It is about a man who tried to help someone. Sadly, he did not help him at all.

The *weather* was very cold. Snow was falling. The roads were covered with ice and a strong wind was *blowing*. It was not a good night to be outside.

Thomas Andrews, however, had to walk home from work. He had

正确——错误

这是一个令人非常难过的故事，是关于一个努力想帮助别人的人的故事。令人悲哀的是，结果却适得其反。

天非常冷，正下着雪，路上结满了冰，风呜呜地吹着，这不是一个适合出门的夜晚。

然而，托马斯·安德鲁下班后不得不沿着乡间小路步行回家。

---

weather *n.* 天气　　　　　　　　　　　　　blow *v.* 刮走；吹

to walk along a country road.

As he walked the cold wind beat against his chest.

"I will be warmer," he thought, "if I wear my coat *backwards*."

He stopped walking for a moment, took off his coat, and put it back on backwards.

"That's much better," he thought, and walked on through the thickly falling snow.

A few minutes later, a car hit him. The driver of the car had not seen him soon enough. When he tried to stop, the car *skidded* on the ice. The driver got out of his car and ran to help Thomas.

Soon a police car arrived. The policeman ran to look at Mr Andrews, who was lying on the ground.

"I'm afraid he's dead," he told the driver.

当他走在路上时，冷风吹打着胸膛。

"如果我把衣服反着穿，"他想："应该更暖和一些。"

他停下来，脱下衣服，反穿在身上。

"这样好多了，"他想，然后继续在纷飞的大雪中前行。

几分钟后一辆车把他撞倒了。司机没能及时看到他，努力想刹车，可车在路面上直打滑。司机从车上跳下来，跑去看看托马斯。

警车也很快到了。警察跑过去查看躺在路上的安德鲁先生。

"恐怕他已经死了。"警察对司机说。

---

backwards *adv.* 向后地

skid *v.* 打滑；滑行

The driver could not believe this.

"He can't be dead," he cried. "I hardly *touched* him. Look at my car. There's not a *mark* on it."

"He's dead," the policeman said. "There is no *doubt*."

"I don't understand it," the driver of the car said. "As soon as I hit him, I ran to help him. He was lying in the road, but he was *breathing* and there was no blood."

"Did you touch him?" the policeman asked.

"Yes," the driver of the car said, "but only to turn his head around the right way."

司机不能接受这一事实。

"他不可能死，"司机喊道："我几乎没有碰到他。看我的车，上面根本没有痕迹。"

"毫无疑问，他死了。"警察对司机说。

"我真不懂，"司机说："我一撞倒他，就跑过去帮他。他当时正躺在路上，喘着气，没有流血。"

"你碰他啦？"警察问道。

"是的，"司机说："我只是把他的头调转到了正确的位置上。"

---

touch v. 触摸

doubt n. 疑问

mark n. 痕迹

breathe v. 呼吸

True Love

Kevin was very much in love with Angela, and he wanted to marry her.

"We have known each other for a year, Angela," he said, "and I want you to be my wife. Will you *marry* me?"

"I don't know, Kevin," Angela said. "A year is not a long time. I don't think I know you very well."

真爱

凯文与安吉拉非常相爱，他很想娶她。

"安吉拉，我们认识已有一年了，"他说，"我想要你做我的妻子。你愿意嫁给我吗？"

"我不知道，凯文，一年时间并不是很长。我想对你的了解还是不够。"安吉拉说。

marry v. 与某人结婚；娶；嫁

18

"What do you want to know?" Kevin asked. "I will answer any questions you like."

"All right," Angela replied. She thought carefully and said, "Here is my first question. Can I always do whatever I want to do?"

"Of course you can *darling*," Kevin said.

"Here is my second question: Can my mother live with us?"

Kevin did not like Angela's mother, but he said, "Of course she can, darling. She can stay *as long as* she wants to."

"Here is my third question," Angela said. "Will you take me shopping every Saturday afternoon?"

Kevin loved playing sports. He was very good at football and swimming. He always played some kind of game on Saturday

---

凯文问："那你想了解些什么呢？我会回答你的任何问题。"

"好吧。"安吉拉回答。她认真思考了一下，说："第一个问题是：我能总做我想做的任何事吗？"

"当然啦，亲爱的。"凯文说。

"第二个问题是：我妈妈能和我们住一起吗？"

凯文并不喜欢安吉拉的母亲，但他依然说，"当然，亲爱的。只要她愿意，住多长时间都行。"

"第三个问题是：你每周六下午都会带我去逛街吗？"安吉拉问道。

凯文热爱运动，足球和游泳是他的强项。以前周六下午他都尝试着各

---

darling *n.* 亲爱的   as long as 只要

afternoons, but he said, "Of course I will darling."

"My last question," Angela said, "is this. Will you stop seeing all your friends and spend all your time with me?"

Kevin had many friends, but he said, "All right darling, if that's what you want. Now, tell me. Will you marry me?"

"No," Angela said.

"Why not?" Kevin asked.

"Because now I know that you are either a *liar* or a *fool*," Angela told him.

种运动项目，但他还是对安吉拉说："是的，亲爱的。"

安吉拉说出了她的最后一个问题："你不再见你的任何朋友，所有时间都和我待在一起，好吗？"

凯文有许多朋友，但他依然说："好的，亲爱的，如果你愿意。现在告诉我，你愿意嫁给我吗？"

"不。"安吉拉说。

"为什么？"凯文百思不得其解。

安吉拉对他说："因为现在我知道了，你不是说谎者就是傻瓜。"

---

liar *n.* 说谎者

fool *n.* 呆子；傻瓜

The Secret of Success

George Wilson had a shop where he sold and repaired watches.

One day his daughter got married. Her husband, James, soon came to work for him.

"I'll teach you everything I know about watches," George told him.

成功的秘密

乔治·威尔森有一家店，出售、维修手表。

一天，他女儿结婚了，她的丈夫詹姆斯不久就到店里帮忙。

乔治告诉他说："我会把我所知道的有关手表的一切都教给你的。"

For the first few weeks, James served customers, *dusted* the *shelves* and learned where everything was in the shop. George was very pleased with him. He worked hard and was polite and helpful to the customers.

While James looked after the front of the shop, George was able to *build up* the repair business. He worked in a back room.

After about six months, James said, "Is there anything else you want to teach me?"

"Yes, James, there is," George said. "It's time I taught you the secret of our success."

"I think I know that," James said. "We buy watches at one price and sell them at a higher price. The difference in price is our *profit*."

"That's true, but it's not where we make most of our profit,"

最初的几周，詹姆斯接待顾客，清扫架子上的灰尘，熟悉店里东西的摆放。乔治对他很满意，他工作努力，对顾客有礼貌，还乐意帮助人。

詹姆斯照看前面店铺时，乔治就在店铺后面维修手表。

大约六个月后，詹姆斯说："还有什么其他你能教我的东西吗？"

"是的，詹姆斯，还有，"乔治说，"现在该教你成功的秘密了。"

詹姆斯说："我知道成功的秘密：我们以一种价格买进手表，再以更高的价格卖出，中间的差价就是我们的利润。"

"是的，但这并不是我们赚取最大利润之所在。"

---

dust *v.* 擦掉灰尘
build up 逐步建立；发展

shelf *n.* （墙上的或橱柜的）搁板；搁架
profit *n.* 利润；赢利

George said.

He picked up a watch from the counter.

"What do you think of this watch?" he asked James.

"That's a cheap watch," the young man replied. "We don't make much money from selling those. *Perhaps* a few dollars each."

"That's where you are wrong, my boy," George said. "These cheap watches make more money than any other watch in the shop."

"I don't understand," James said.

"Because they are really cheap, they are always *breaking*," George told him. "We make our profit from repairing them."

他从柜台上拿起一块手表问詹姆斯："你觉得这块表怎么样？"

"那是块廉价的手表，"年轻人回答说，"卖那种表根本赚不了多少钱，每块表只赚几美元。"

乔治说："这你就错了，孩子。这些廉价的手表比店里其他任何手表赚的钱都多。"

"我真不明白，"詹姆斯说。

"因为它们实在太廉价了，所以经常坏掉，"乔治告诉他，"维修费才是我们真正利润之所在。"

---

perhaps *adv.* 或许；可能　　　　　　break *v.* 出故障；损坏

Almost Sure

William White was a very *bad-tempered* man. He was always shouting at people. He worked in an office and his *staff* hated him.

His secretary, Rachel, had the worst time. She had to work with him all day, and he was often very *rude* to her.

"I don't know how you *put up with* him all day," one of her friends

---

对号入座

威廉·怀特脾气特别暴躁，总对人大喊大叫。他在办公室工作，员工都很讨厌他。

他的秘书拉切尔的日子最不好过了，不得不整天和他在一起，而他常对她很不客气。

"我真不知道你整天是怎么忍受他的，"和拉切尔一个办公室的朋友说，"他对你太不客气了。"

---

bad-tempered *adj.* 脾气坏的；易怒的
rude *adj.* 无礼的；粗鲁的

staff *n.* 全体职工；全体雇员
put up with 忍受；容忍

in the office said. "He's so impolite to you."

"One day I'll teach him a lesson," Rachel said. "I'll make him look *foolish* in front of everyone."

A few weeks later, Rachel spoke to her friend again. "I've got an idea," she said, "but I need your help." She told her friend her idea.

"That's a great idea," her friend said. "We'll do it tomorrow between eleven and twelve o'clock. I'll wait until the office is quiet, so everybody will hear you speak to him."

The next morning William White's telephone rang at 11:15. As usual, Rachel answered it for him.

"Mr White's secretary speaking," she said.

"总有一天我要教训教训他，" 拉切尔说，"我要让他在众人面前出丑。"

几周后，拉切尔再次对她朋友说："我有主意了，但我需要你的帮助。"她把想法告诉了朋友。

"真是个好主意，"她朋友说，"明天11点到12点之间吧，我会等到办公室最安静的时候，这样每个人都能听到你对他说的话了。"

第二天上午11:15，威廉·怀特的电话响了起来，跟往常一样，拉切尔接电话。

"我是怀特先生的秘书，"她说。

---

foolish *adj.* 愚蠢的

Everyone in the office stopped work and looked at her. There was *total* silence in the room.

"Just a minute please," Rachel said.

She turned to William White.

"Excuse me Mr White, but I think there's a call for you," she said.

"Think?" William White shouted. "Think? Think? You're not paid to think! Why don't you know, you stupid woman?"

"Well sir," Rachel said, "the caller did not ask for you by name. He just said, 'Is that bad-tempered old fool in the office?'"

大家都停下手中的工作，办公室一片寂静。

拉切尔说："请稍等，"她转向威廉·怀特说："打扰一下，怀特先生，我认为有电话找你。"

"认为？"威廉·怀特喊道，"认为？认为？我付你薪水不是让你'认为'的！你为什么就不知道呢，你这愚蠢的女人？"

"先生，"拉切尔说，"打电话的人没有说出你的名字，只是说'那个坏脾气的老傻瓜在办公室吗？'"

---

total *adj.* 完全的；全部的

9

The Twins

A man had two sons. They were twins. They looked exactly alike, but in one important way they were very different: One was an *optimist*, while the other one was a *pessimist*.

An optimist is someone who always thinks that good things will happen. A pessimist is someone who always thinks that bad things will happen.

The man was worried about his sons. There are good and bad

双胞胎

一人有两个儿子，是双胞胎，虽然相貌非常相像，但有一点却截然不同：一个是乐观主义者，另一个是悲观主义者。

乐观主义者是那种总认为会有好事发生的人，而悲观主义者则是总认为有坏事发生的人。

这个人对两个儿子忧心忡忡，因为他知道生活中既有好事也有坏事，

---

optimist *n.* 乐观的人；乐观主义者　　　　pessimist *n.* 悲观的人；悲观主义者

things in life, he knew. He did not want them to be too pessimistic or too optimistic. He took his problem to a friend, Sally.

"How can I *cure* them of their foolish optimism and pessimism?" he asked his friend.

Sally was thoughtful. Then she said, "When is their next birthday?"

"It's on Wednesday," the father replied. "They'll be twelve years old."

"*Excellent*," Sally said. "Here's what you should do. Give your pessimistic son a really wonderful present. Give your optimistic son a really terrible present. That should cure them of their optimism and pessimism."

不想他们太过悲观或太过乐观。他带着这个问题找到了朋友萨丽。

"我怎么帮他们克服那愚蠢的乐观和悲观呢？"他问。

萨丽沉思了一会儿，然后说："他们什么时候过生日？"

"周三，"这位父亲回答说，"他们将满12岁了。"

"太棒了，"萨丽说，"你这样，送一份非常珍贵的礼物给悲观的儿子，一份不怎么好的礼物给乐观的儿子。这样他们就能克服乐观和悲观了。"

---

cure *v.* 治疗；治愈 　　　　　　　　　excellent *adj.* 极好的

The father did as his friend told him.

The next Wednesday morning the boys looked at their birthday presents.

The pessimist looked at his first. It was a beautiful and very expensive gold watch, but he was not pleased with it.

"Awww," he said, "I don't like this very much. I'm sure it won't keep good time. It will always be fast or slow, and it will probably break many times, and I'll have to spend lots of money to get it repaired."

Then the optimist looked at his present. He was really pleased.

"Look! Dad's given me a *shoelace*," he said. He held up the shoelace.

"I haven't found the shoes yet, but I'm sure they are here somewhere."

父亲照办了。

周三上午，两个孩子看到了生日礼物。

悲观的儿子先看到了他的礼物，是块非常漂亮、非常昂贵的金表，但他对此一点也不满意。

"哎呀，"他说，"我一点也不喜欢这礼物。我敢肯定它走时不准，要么快要么慢，而且可能会经常坏掉，我还得花很多钱去修。"

接下来，乐观的儿子看到了他的礼物，非常高兴。

"看哪！爸爸送了我鞋带，"边说边举起了这根鞋带。

"我还没找到鞋呢，但我敢肯定鞋一定是藏在什么地方了。"

---

shoelace *n.* 鞋带

The Bet

 One day June Smith visited the family doctor, Edward Swain. Doctor Swain was an old man with a long *beard*.

"What's the problem, June?" doctor Swain asked her.

"I'm very worried about my son, Teddy," June said. "I can't stop him from *gambling*. He spends all his

---

打赌

　　一天，朱恩·史密斯去拜访他的家庭医生爱得华·斯温，斯温医生是位留着长胡子的老人。

　　"你有什么不舒服吗？" 斯温医生问她。

　　"我非常担心儿子泰迪，"朱恩说，"我没法阻止他赌博，他把所有的钱都花在赌马上了，不仅仅是赌马，任何事情他都赌，无论是什么。"

---

beard *n.* 胡须；络腮胡子　　　　　　　　　　　gamble *v.* 赌；赌博

money *betting* on horse races. And not just on horse races. He'll bet on anything. It doesn't matter what it is."

"I've cured people of gambling before," doctor Swain said. "Send him to me. I'll talk to him."

A week later doctor Swain spoke to Mrs Smith on the phone.

"I think I've cured your son," he said.

"That's wonderful. How did you do it?"

"Well," the doctor said, "it was very strange. While we were talking he was looking at my beard. Suddenly he said, 'I'll bet you $50 that's a false beard.'"

"Oh, no!" June said.

"It's all right," the doctor said. "I knew what to do. 'My beard isn't

---

"我以前治好过嗜赌的人，" 斯温医生说，"把他送过来吧，我跟他聊聊。"

一周后，斯温医生和史密斯太太通了电话。

"我想我已经治好了你的儿子，"他说。

"太棒了，你怎么治好的呢？"

医生说："这有点古怪，聊天时他一直盯着我胡子，然后突然说：'我赌50美元，你的胡子是假的。'"

"噢，不！"朱恩喊道。

"没关系，"医生说，"我知道该这么办。我告诉他说'我的胡子不

---

bet *v.* 下赌注；与……打赌 　　　　　　　　false *adj.* 不真实的；假的

a *false* one,' I told him. 'And I can prove it.'"

"'Can I pull your beard and find out?' your son asked me."

"I thought this was my chance to teach him a *lesson*, so I said, 'Yes, you can pull my beard.'"

"Well, he pulled it, and soon *found out* it was real." The doctor laughed. "He had to pay me $50. That should cure his gambling."

"Doctor," Mrs Smith said. "You're wrong. You haven't cured him. You've made him worse."

"How can that be?"

"The day before he went to see you, he bet me $100 that you would ask him to pull your beard!"

是假的，我可以证明。' "

"你的儿子问我，'我可以拽你的胡子看看吗？' "

"我觉得这是我教训他的一个好机会，就说，'行啊，你可以拽我的胡子。' "

"他拽了，然后发现胡子是真的，" 医生笑道，"他不得不给我50美元，这应该能治好他赌博的毛病。"

"医生，" 史密斯太太说，"你错了，你没有治好他，反而使情况更糟了。

"怎么会呢？"

"他去见你的前一天，就跟我赌100美元说你会让他拽胡子的！"

---

lesson *n.* 教训；训诫   find out 发现

The Cure

Patsy was in the hospital. Her friend Mary went to see her. Mary found her lying in bed, *wrapped* in *bandages*.

"Patsy!" Mary said. "What happened to you?"

"When I woke up this morning," Patsy said, "I had a headache."

"A headache?"

治病

佩茜住院了，朋友玛丽去探望。玛丽看到她躺在床上，浑身缠着绷带。

"佩茜！"玛丽喊道，"你怎么啦？"

"早晨醒来的时候有点头疼。"佩茜说。

"头疼？"

---

wrap *v.* 包；裹   bandage *n.* 绷带

"Yes. So I went to see the doctor."

"You look as if you've broken every bone in your body!" Mary said.

"I know, and I have, well almost."

"How did it happen?"

"Well, I told my doctor about my headache, and he said I needed more exercise, so I went for a walk in the park."

"The park isn't dangerous," Mary said. "It's beautiful there."

"Well, yes, but as I was looking up at a bird in a tree ,I *tripped* and fell down. I *twisted* my *ankle* and couldn't walk. Someone called an *ambulance*."

"But you don't need all those bandages for a twisted ankle," Mary said.

"嗯，所以来看医生了。"

"可你看起来好像全身的每一块骨头都碎了！"

"我知道，我几乎……嗯……所有的骨头都碎了。"

"怎么回事啊？"

"我告诉医生头疼，他说我需要多多锻炼，所以我去公园散步。"

"公园并不危险，那儿很美啊。"

"嗯，可正当我抬头看树上的小鸟时摔倒了，扭伤了脚踝不能走路，有人就叫了救护车。"

"就算脚踝扭伤也不需要这么多绷带啊。"玛丽说

---

trip *v.* 绊倒

ankle *n.* 踝关节；踝节部

twist *v.* 扭；拧；盘绕

ambulance *n.* 救护车

"Oh, I know that," Patsy said. "The problem was that the ambulance men put me on a *stretcher*. Then as they were lifting me into the ambulance, I fell off the stretcher and broke my leg."

"But why do you have bandages around your arm?" Mary asked.

"Well, when I got to the hospital, the doctor gave me some medicine to stop the pain in my leg and I fell asleep. *Unfortunately*, he made a mistake with my name."

"And another doctor *operated* on your arm!" Mary said.

"That's right," Patsy said. "But I shouldn't *complain*. My doctor was right. The walk in the park was good for me: My headache is completely gone now."

"哦，我知道，"佩茜说，"问题是救护人员把我放到担架上，抬去救护车时，我从担架上掉下来摔断了腿。"

"可为什么胳膊上还缠着绷带呢？"玛丽问。

"我到医院时，医生在腿部敷了些止痛药，接着我就睡着了。不幸的是，他把我名字弄错了。"

"另一个医生给你胳膊做手术了？"玛丽说。

"是这样的，"佩茜说，"但我不应该抱怨。医生是对的，在公园里散步对我的确有好处：我的头现在已经不疼了。"

---

stretcher *n.* 担架
operate *v.* 动手术

unfortunately *adv.* 不幸的；遗憾的
complain *v.* 抱怨

12

Information Please

The hospital was very busy. The nurses hurried from *patient* to patient. They did not have time to talk with the patients or answer their questions. Instead they just gave them their medicines, made their beds and moved on.

The head nurse was as busy as the other nurses. She had to

打听

医院里很忙，护士们忙着从这个病床跑到那个病床，没有时间和患者交谈或回答他们的问题，只是分发药品，整理床铺，然后就走开了。

护士长和其他护士一样繁忙，她必须和医生一起到处巡查，确保护士们都很好地完成本职工作，完成她的报告，还要接电话。

---

patient *n.* 病人

walk around with the doctors, make sure the nurses were doing their work, complete her *reports* and answer the phone.

Many of the phone calls were from the friends and relatives of the patients. They were telephoning for information about the people in the hospital.

One phone call, however, was a little different from all the others.

The phone rang and the head nurse answered it. "Hello," she said.

At the other end of the line a voice replied, "Good morning. I'm phoning about Fred Williams. Could you tell me how he is please?"

The head nurse looked at her *notes* and said, "Mr Williams has had his operation, and is now resting."

"Can you tell me if his *condition* is good?" the voice asked.

"Yes," the head nurse replied. "He is *comfortable*; his operation

---

很多电话都是患者的亲戚和朋友打来的，都是想打听病人的情况。

但是，有一个电话和其他的电话不太一样。

电话铃响了，护士长接起来："你好。"

电话另一端的声音回答："早上好，我想了解弗雷德·威廉姆斯的情况，你能告诉我他现在怎么样了吗？"

护士长看了看记录说："威廉姆斯先生刚刚做完手术，正在休息。"

"他的情况还好吧？"这声音问道。

"不错，"护士长回答说，"他感觉不错，手术很成功。"

---

report *n.* 报道；报告
condition *n.* 现状；状况

note *n.* 笔记；记录
comfortable *adj.* 舒适的

was a *success*."

"When do you think he will be able to go home?" the voice asked.

"Oh, probably at the end of the week," the head nurse said. Then she asked, "May I tell him who is asking about him?"

"Yes," the voice replied. "Fred Williams."

"No, that's the patient's name," the head nurse said.

"Yes. I am the patient. Phoning you is the only way I can get any information about my condition."

"你认为他什么时候能回家？"这声音问道。

"哦，大概周末吧，"护士长说，接着她又问："我能告诉他是谁在询问他的病情吗？"

"是的，"对方回答说，"弗雷德·威廉姆斯。"

"不，那是患者的名字，"护士长说。

"是的，我就是患者。给你打电话是我能够打听到病情的唯一办法。"

---

success *n.* 成功   probably *adv.* 大概；很可能

13

The Price of Steak

Tom was a *shopkeeper*. He had a small *corner* shop. It was open from seven in the morning until eleven at night and sold many different things. Tom worked hard in his shop but he had a good business and he was happy.

Then a supermarket opened across the street. The supermarket was ten times the size of Tom's shop. The *manager* of the supermarket wanted to take Tom's customers

牛排的价格

汤姆是一家街角小店的店主，小店从早晨7点一直营业到晚上11点，出售许多不同种类的商品。汤姆在店里工作很辛苦，但生意还不错，因此他很开心。

后来街对面开了一家超市，有汤姆小店的十倍大。超市的经理想把汤姆的顾客抢过来，于是弄清了汤姆店里商品的价格，超市的价格就定得比他低。

shopkeeper *n.* 店主
manager *n.* 经理

corner *n.* 角落；拐角处

away from him. He found out what Tom's prices were and then made his *lower* than Tom's.

People quickly stopped buying things from Tom's shop. They bought everything from the supermarket instead. Soon Tom's business was very bad and he was angry.

"It's not fair," Tom thought. "I must do something to teach that supermarket manager a lesson."

The price of steak in the supermarket was $5 a pound. Tom put a sign in his window, "Steak. 4 point 50 dollars a *pound*."

The next day the price of steak in the supermarket was 4 point 25 dollars a pound. Tom changed the sign in his window. "Steak. $4 a pound."

An hour later, the sign in the supermarket said, "Steak. 3 point 75 dollars a pound." Ten minutes later the sign in Tom's window said,

---

很快人们就不在汤姆店里买东西，而是在超市买东西。不久汤姆的生意变得很不景气，这令他非常生气。

"这不公平，"汤姆想，"我必须给超市经理一个教训。"

超市牛排的价格是每磅5美元，汤姆在橱窗放了一个标牌，"牛排——每磅4.5美元。"

第二天超市牛排的价格变成每磅4.25美元，汤姆将标牌换成"牛排——每磅4美元。"

一小时后，超市的标牌上写着"牛排——每磅3.75美元。"10分钟后

---

low *adj.* 低的；矮的   pound *n.* 磅

"Steak. 3point 50 dollars a pound."

Five minutes later the sign in the supermarket said, "Steak. 2 point 50 dollars a pound." Twenty seconds later the sign in Tom's window said, "Steak. $1 a pound."

The manager of the supermarket ran across the road into Tom's shop. "This price cutting must stop," he said. "Steak is costing me $4 a pound. I'm selling it at 2 point 50 dollars a pound. I'm losing money every minute!"

"I'll stop cutting all my prices," Tom said, "if you will stop cutting all yours."

The supermarket manager agreed, and the two men shook hands.

Tom smiled. He had not lost any money on steak. He did not sell steak.

汤姆店橱窗的标牌写着"牛排——每磅3.5美元。"

5分钟后超市的标牌上写着"牛排——每磅2.5美元。"20秒后汤姆店橱窗的标牌上写着"牛排——每磅1美元。"

超市的经理跑到汤姆店里，说："这种降价必须停止，我以每磅4美元的价格买进牛排，现在以每磅2.5美元的价格销售，每分钟都在赔钱！"

"如果你停止商品的降价，"汤姆说，"我也会的。"

超市经理同意了，两人握手言和。

汤姆笑了，他没在牛排上赔钱，因为店里根本就不卖牛排。

Catch of the Day

Tom Jenkins enjoyed fishing and spent most of his time by the river.

He enjoyed being in the *fresh* air and being on his own. There was no one to trouble him and the time passed happily for him.

Unfortunately, he was not a very

一天的钓鱼量

汤姆·詹金斯喜欢钓鱼，大部分时间都待在河边。

他喜欢一个人呼吸新鲜空气，没人烦扰，时间对他来说过得很愉快。

不幸的是，他并不是一个很好的垂钓手，他要么是在错误的地方钓鱼，使用错误的鱼饵，要么就是拽线太快了。无论是什么原因，他从没钓

---

fresh *adj.* 新鲜的

good fisherman. He either fished in the wrong place, used the wrong bait or pulled in his line too quickly. Whatever the reason, he never caught anything big enough to eat.

However, he did not like to admit this to his wife. He thought she would complain if she knew he was wasting his time. She would try to stop him from going fishing. She might even make him take her shopping!

It was very important to Tom, therefore, that she thought that he was a good fisherman.

For this reason, on the way home from the river he always visited the *local* fish shop and bought something. Then he told his wife he had caught it and they had a good fish for their dinner.

One evening, after yet, another day's unsuccessful fishing, Tom

---

到过大一些，可以吃的鱼。

但是，他从不愿意对妻子承认这一点，他认为如果妻子知道他在浪费时间，她会抱怨的，她会竭力阻止他再去钓鱼的，她甚至会让他带她去购物！

因此，对汤姆来说让妻子认为他是个好垂钓手是很重要的。

为了这个原因，在从河边回家的路上，他总是去当地的鱼店去买些什么，然后他告诉他的妻子是他钓的鱼，他们可以有条大鱼当晚餐了。

一天傍晚，在一整天失败的垂钓后，汤姆和往常一样在回家的路上停

---

local *adj.* 当地的；地方的

stopped at the fish shop as usual on his way home.

"I'll have three *perch* please," he said to the shopkeeper.

"And throw them to me, as usual, so I can tell my wife I caught them."

The shopkeeper laughed and said, "I suggest you take a nice *salmon* instead."

"Oh why?" Tom asked.

"Your wife came in an hour ago and said, 'When Tom comes in, make sure he 'catches' a salmon.'"

在了那家鱼店。

"请给我来三条鲈鱼，"他对店主说。

"老规矩，将它们扔给我，这样我可以告诉我妻子是我抓的鱼。"

店主笑着说："我建议你买一条上好的三文鱼吧。"

"哦，为什么？"汤姆问道。

"一小时前你妻子来说，'汤姆来时，让他'钓'一条三文鱼。'"

---

perch *n.* 鲈鱼

salmon *n.* 鲑鱼，三文鱼

15

A Short Holiday

Alan worked in an office in the city. He worked very hard and really looked forward to his holidays.

He usually went to the *seaside*, but one year he saw an advertisement in a newspaper. "Enjoy country life. Spend a few weeks at Willow Farm. Good food. Fresh air. Horseback riding. Walking. Fishing. Great prices."

"This sounds like a good idea," he thought. "I'll spend a month

短期休假

艾伦在办公室工作，非常辛苦，一直期盼着假期的来临。

他通常去海边度假，但有一年他看到报纸上的一则广告，"享受乡村生活。在维罗农场待上几周，美味的食物、新鲜的空气、骑马、散步、钓鱼。价格优惠。"

"这听起来不错啊，"他想，"我将在维罗农场待一个月，我要好好享受骑马、散步和钓鱼的乐趣。这和在海边感觉是完全不同的。"

seaside *n.* 海滨

at Willow Farm. I'll enjoy horseback riding, walking and fishing. It'll make a change from sitting by the seaside."

He wrote to the farmer and *arranged* to spend all of July on the farm. Then, on the first of July, he left for Willow Farm.

Four days later he returned home.

"What was wrong with Willow Farm?" his friend, Jack, asked him. "Didn't you enjoy country life?"

"Country life was fine," Alan said. "But there was another problem."

"Oh? What?"

"Well," he explained, "the first day I was there a sheep died, and we had *roast lamb* for dinner."

他给农场主写信，说整个7月都要待在农场，7月1号，他动身去了维罗农场。

四天后他就回了家。

"维罗农场有什么不好的地方吗？"朋友杰克问，"你不喜欢乡村生活吗？"

"乡村生活还不错，"艾伦说，"但有其他的问题。"

"哦，怎么啦？"

他解释说："我在那里的第一天，一头羊死了，于是我们晚餐吃烤羊肉。"

---

arrange *v.* 安排；准备
lamb *n.* 羊羔

roast *adj.* 烤好的；烤制的

"What's wrong with that?" Jack asked. "Fresh meat is the best."

"I know, but on the second day a cow died, and we had roast beef for dinner."

"Lucky you!"

"You don't understand," Alan said, "On the third day a pig died and we had roast pork for dinner."

"A different roast every day," Jack *exclaimed*, "and you're complaining!"

"Let me finish," Alan said. "On the fourth day the farmer's wife died, and I didn't *dare* stay for dinner!"

"那有什么问题呢？"杰克问，"新鲜的肉最好吃了。"

"我知道，但第二天一头牛死了，于是我们晚餐吃了烤牛肉。"

"你真幸运！"

"你还不明白，"艾伦说，"第三天，一头猪死了，我们晚餐吃了烤猪肉。"

"每天都有不同的烤肉呀，"杰克欢呼道，"可你竟然还抱怨！"

"让我说完，"艾伦说，"第四天，农场主的妻子死了，我再不敢待在那里吃晚餐了！"

---

exclaim *v.* 呼喊

dare *v.* 敢；敢于

26

A Free Meal

"**I'm** hungry," Pat said to his friend Mike. "Let's have a meal somewhere."

They walked down the road until they came to an expensive restaurant.

"This will be fine," Pat said. "Just the place we want."

He opened the door and they went inside. The head waiter came

---

免费午餐

"我饿了，"帕特对朋友迈克说，"咱们找个地方吃饭吧。"

他们沿路向下走，来到一家昂贵的餐馆。

"这不错啊，"帕特说，"正是我们想去的地方。"

他推开门，走了进去。领班立刻朝他们走过来。

MCGRAW-HILL

up to them immediately.

"A table for two , gentlemen?" he asked.

"Yes. The best table you have."

He took them to a table near a window. He handed them the menu and went away.

Pat and Mike looked at the menu carefully, then ordered the most expensive dishes and a bottle of very good *wine*.

An hour later, they had almost finished their meals. It was one of the best meals they had ever had, and now they were eating their *dessert*. Suddenly Pat looked carefully at his dish.

"What's this?" he cried, *pointing* at something small and black in the dessert. The head waiter hurried towards their table.

"两位吗，先生？"他问。

"对，挑最好的位置。"

领班将他们带到临窗的位置，递上菜单就走开了。

帕特和迈克仔细看了菜单，点了最贵的菜和上好的葡萄酒。

一小时后，他们快吃完了，这是他们吃过的最好的午餐之一，接着他们开始吃甜点。突然，帕特仔细盯着菜。

"这是什么？"他喊道，指着甜品中又黑又小的东西。领班立刻走过来。

---

wine *n.* 葡萄酒

point *v.* (用手指、棍等)指；指向

dessert *n.* 甜食；甜点心

"Look at this!" Pat said to him in a very loud voice. "There's a dead *fly* in my dessert. How terrible! I thought this was a good restaurant, but I was wrong."

The head waiter was very *embarrassed*. "Please, sir, do not speak so loud. You will upset the other customers. I am very sorry about the fly. I'm afraid *accidents* happen sometimes, even in the best restaurants. We will not, of course, charge you for your meals."

Soon after this, Mike and Pat were walking past a hotel.

"Let's go in and have a drink," Pat said. "I've got one fly left."

"看看这个！"帕特扯大嗓门说，"甜品中有一只死苍蝇。太可怕了！我还以为这是家最好的餐馆呢，但我错了。"

领班非常尴尬，"先生，请不要这样大声说话，会打扰其他顾客的。对苍蝇一事我非常抱歉，恐怕即使在最好的餐馆，有时也会有意外发生。当然了，这顿饭免单了。"

从餐馆出来不久，迈克和帕特路过一家酒店。

"咱们进去喝点儿什么吧，"帕特说，"我这里还剩一只苍蝇。"

---

fly *n.* 苍蝇　　　　　　　　embarrassed *adj.* 难堪的；尴尬的
accident *n.* 意外事件；事故

50

17

The Bird

There were three brothers, John, Jack and James. Every year on their mother's birthday, they sent her expensive presents. They liked to show her how rich and successful they were.

The oldest brother, John, had the most money and he wanted his mother to know this.

"I must give her something *neither* of my brothers can give her,"

鸟

有三个兄弟，分别叫约翰、杰克和詹姆斯。每年妈妈过生日时，他们都会给她寄昂贵的礼物，他们喜欢向她表明自己有多富有多成功。

大哥约翰最有钱，他想让妈妈知道这一点。

"我必须送给她两个弟弟都不能给的东西，"约翰想，"我必须找到整个世界上独一无二的东西。"

---

neither *pron.* （二者）都不

John thought. "I must find something of which there is only one in the whole world."

He advertised in the newspapers. "Wanted. The *perfect gift* for the woman who has everything."

For many days his telephone did not stop ringing. People phoned him from all over the world. They wanted to sell him "the perfect gift." However, they did not have anything that was the only one in the whole world.

Then, less than a week before his mother's birthday, a man came to his office. He was carrying a *cage*, and in the cage there was a large bird.

"This bird," the man said, "can speak ten languages and sing any *pop song*. There is no other bird like it in the world."

"I will listen to it," John said. "If you are telling the truth, I will buy

---

他在报纸上登广告，"寻求一份送给一位拥有一切的女人的完美礼物。"

许多天来，他的电话一直响个不停，世界各地的人们都打来电话，想卖给他"完美的礼物"。但是他们并没有世界上仅此一件的东西。

不久，在妈妈生日前一周，一个人来到了他办公室，手拿着一个笼子，笼子里有一只大鸟。

"这只鸟，"此人说，"能讲10种语言，会唱任何流行歌曲，世界上再没有像它这样的鸟了。"

"我倒要听听，"约翰说，"如果你说的是真的，我就买了。"

---

perfect *adj.* 完美的；无瑕的
cage *n.* 笼子

gift *n.* 礼物
pop song 流行音乐；流行歌曲

the bird from you."

The man spoke to the bird. "Talk to me in French," he said. The bird spoke to him in French. "Tell me a joke in Japanese," he said. The bird told him a joke in Japanese. "Sing a famous pop song," he said. The bird sang a famous pop song.

"I'll buy it," John said. "How much do you want?"

"One hundred thousand dollars," the man said. This was a lot of money but John paid him. Then he sent the bird to his mother with a birthday card.

The day after his mother's birthday he phoned her. "Well, mother," he said, "what did you think of the bird?"

"Oh, it was *delicious*, dear," she said.

此人对那鸟说："用法语跟我讲话。"那鸟就说法语。"用日语给我讲个笑话，"他说，那鸟就讲日语。"唱一首著名的流行歌曲，"他说，那鸟就唱了一首著名的流行歌曲。

"我买它了，"约翰说，"多少钱？"

"100,000美元，"那人说。虽然很贵，但约翰还是付了钱。接着他把这只鸟连同一张生日卡一同寄给了妈妈。

第二天，他给妈妈打电话，"妈妈，那只鸟怎么样啊？"

"哦，它味道好极了，亲爱的。"妈妈说。

---

delicious *adj.* 美味的；可口的

18

A Generous Gift

A woman was *collecting* money for a *church charity*. The money she collected was going to be given to poor *orphans*. children who had no parents to take care of them.

She went from apartment to apartment and from house to house. She knocked on doors and asked for money.

慷慨的礼物

　　一位女士正在为教堂的慈善事业筹集款项，这笔钱将送给可怜的孤儿——那些没有父母照顾的孩子。

　　她从一家公寓走到另一家公寓，从一栋房子走到另一栋房子，敲门募集钱。

---

collect *v.* 募集（捐款）　　　　　　church *n.* 教堂

charity *n.* 慈善团体　　　　　　　orphan *n.* 孤儿

She always said the same thing.

"Good morning, I'm collecting for a church charity. Please give *generously*. We need $5000 to help poor orphans."

Then she held out a collection box. Most people put a few *coins* in.

An artist lived in one of the apartments. He opened the door when she knocked one morning.

"Good morning," she said. "I'm collecting for a church charity. Please give generously. We need $5000 to help poor orphans."

The artist thought for a moment, then he said, "I'm sorry, but I don't have any money. However, I'll give you a painting. It's worth $400."

她总是说同样的话。

"早上好，我在为教堂的慈善事业筹钱呢，请慷慨地施与吧，我们需要5000美元来帮助那些可怜的孤儿。"

然后她拿出募捐箱，大部分人都会往里放几枚硬币。

一位艺术家住在一个公寓里，这天早晨，她敲开了他房门。

"早上好，"她说，"我在为教堂的慈善事业筹钱，请慷慨地施与吧，我们需要5000美元来帮助那些可怜的孤儿。"

这位艺术家想了一会儿，说："很抱歉，我没有钱，但我会给你一幅画，它值400美元。"

---

generously *adv.* 慷慨地；大方地

coin *n.* 硬币

The woman thanked the artist and took the painting away.

A week later she called on him again.

"I'm sorry to trouble you again," she said, "but we still need more money. We need another $100. Can you help?"

"Of course," the artist said. "I'll *increase* the value of my painting to $500."

这位女士谢过艺术家，拿着画走了。

一周后，她再次拜访了艺术家。

"很抱歉再次打扰您，"她说，"但是我们还差一点钱，还需要100美元，你能帮忙吗？"

"当然了，"艺术家说，"把我那幅画的价格提高到500美元吧。"

---

increase *v.* 增长；增强

Magic

Some children were sitting in English class.

"This week," the teacher said, "I want you to write a story about your family. I want you to tell me about your parents and your brothers and sisters."

Lisa *raised* her hand.

"What kind of thing can I write about my father?" she asked.

魔术

一群孩子在上英语课。

"这一周，"老师说，"我要求你们写一篇关于你家庭的故事，你们得告诉我有关父母和兄弟姐妹的事情。"

丽萨举起了手。

"我要写关于爸爸的什么事呢？"她问。

---

raise *v.* 举起；抬起

"Well," the teacher said. "Write about his work. What does your father do?"

"He's a *magician*," Lisa said.

"A magician! How interesting," the teacher said. "Does he do *magic tricks* on *stage*?"

"Yes," Lisa said, "He's been on television too. He's a famous magician."

The teacher was very interested in this. "Tell the class something about him," she said. "What is his most difficult trick?"

"嗯，"老师说，"写他的工作吧，你爸爸是做什么的？"

"他是位魔术师，"丽萨说。

"魔术师！太有意思了！"老师说，"他在舞台上表演魔术戏法吗？"

"是的，"丽萨说，"他还上过电视呢，是位著名的魔术师。"

老师对此非常感兴趣，"给全班同学讲讲他吧，"她说，"他表演的最难的戏法是什么？"

---

magician *n.* 魔术师   magic trick 魔术；戏法
stage *n.* 舞台

Lisa thought for a moment and said, "He *saws* people in half. He puts them in a large box and then saws the box in half."

"That's a very clever trick," the teacher said. "I'm sure he must practice it a lot."

"Yes, he does," Lisa said.

Then the teacher asked her, "Who else is in your family?"

"There's my mother," Lisa said, "and I've got a half-brother and two half-sisters."

丽萨想了一会儿，说道，"把人锯成两半。他把人放进大箱子里，然后将箱子锯成两半。"

"那戏法真是太妙了，"老师说，"我肯定他一定练习了好多次。"

"是的，的确如此，"丽萨说。

老师接着问："你家里还有什么人？"

"还有我妈妈，"丽萨说，"还有一个两半的弟弟和两个两半的妹妹。"（此处为幽默用法）

---

saw *v.* 锯；拉锯

Helping Hands

Jane Warner's husband, Jack, was sent to *prison* for two years for stealing. While he was in prison, Jane had a very difficult time.

She had two children, but no job.

Her husband, of course, did not make any money either. The only money she got was a small *amount* from the *government*.

援助之手

简·华纳的丈夫杰克因偷窃被送到监狱服刑两年，丈夫入狱期间，生活对简来说非常艰难。

她有两个孩子，都没有工作。

当然，她丈夫也赚不了钱，她所能拿到的唯一一笔钱就是政府的补助。

prison *n.* 监狱
government *n.* 政府

amount *n.* 数量；数额

"I don't know how we will *manage*," she wrote to her husband in prison. "I get only enough money to pay the rent. There isn't enough money for food. I think I'll have to plant vegetables in the garden. They'll grow quickly. We can live on vegetables."

The garden was quite large, and much of it was covered with grass.

When Jack Warner received his wife's letter, he replied to it immediately.

"Don't *dig* up the garden," he wrote. "That's where the money I stole is hidden."

All letters written by the prisoners were read by one of the *guards* before they were mailed. When the guard read Jack's letter, he telephoned the police. He told them what Jack had written to his wife.

"我不知道该怎么活下去，"她写信给狱中的丈夫，"我拿到的钱只够付房租，没有钱吃饭。我得在花园里种些蔬菜，等它们长大就可以靠蔬菜生活了。"

花园很大，大部分地方都覆盖着青草。

当杰克·华纳收到妻子信时，立刻就回了信。

"不要挖花园，"他说，"我偷来的钱都藏在那里了。"

所有囚犯写的信在寄走之前都要给警卫读一遍。当警卫读到杰克的信时，他给警察打了电话，告诉了警察杰克写信的内容。

---

manage *v.* 设法；做成   dig *v.* 挖；刨
guard *n.* 警卫；看守

The police immediately went to Jack's house. They took *pitchforks* and *shovels* with them. They dug up the garden, looking for the money, but they did not find anything.

When they had gone, Mrs Warner wrote to her husband.

"The police came today," she wrote. "They dug up all the grass. What should I do?"

Her husband wrote back immediately, "Plant the vegetables."

警察立刻赶到了杰克家，带着干草叉和铁锹，挖开了花园找钱，但什么也没找到。

当他们走后，华纳太太给丈夫写信。

"今天警察来了，"她写道，"他们把所有的草都挖开了，我该怎么办？"

她丈夫立刻回信道，"种蔬菜。"

---

pitchfork *n.* 干草叉；长柄草耙   shovel *n.* 铲子；铁锹

21

Losing Things

Aman named Nick went on a fishing holiday. Fishing was his favorite sport, and he had many prizes for fish he had caught.

One summer the weather was beautiful and the fishing *was supposed* to be good, so he decided to travel around the country,

---

失去的东西

一个叫尼克的人整个假期都花在钓鱼上了。钓鱼是他最喜欢的运动，他也因所钓到的鱼获得了很多殊荣。

夏季的一天，天气很好，钓鱼应该是件非常愉快的事情，因此他决定绕着乡下旅行，在每一条河里都花些时间钓鱼。

---

be supposed to 应该；被期望

spending a few days fishing in each of the rivers.

Unfortunately, he didn't have much luck, and he caught only a few small fish. He was quite *disappointed* and was going to go back home, when he heard of a large river that was full of fish nearby.

He found the river quite easily and followed it through the country to a place where it *flowed* through a farm. He decided to ask the farmer's *permission* to fish in the river.

"You have my permission," the farmer said, "but you should be careful. For years I stopped my kids from going near that river."

"Is the river dangerous?" Nick asked.

"It's not the river," the farmer said, "it's the fish. They're *huge*. They're so big that my kids couldn't hold them."

可惜他运气不好，只钓到了一些小鱼。他很失望，正准备回家时听说附近有一条大河里鱼很多。

他很快就找到了那条河，沿着河流来到了一个农场。他决定争取农民的允许来这里钓鱼。

"我允许了，"农民说，"但是你要小心，我多年都不许我的孩子靠近那条河。"

"那条河很危险吗？"尼克问。

"不是河危险，"农民说，"是鱼。它们很大，我的孩子都抓不住它们。

---

disappointed *adj.* 失望的；沮丧的
permission *n.* 允许；准许

flow *v.* 流动
huge *adj.* 巨大的；庞大的

Nick was very excited. All fishermen want to catch really big fish.

"How big are they?" he asked.

"Well," the farmer told him, "last week I *lost* one over three feet long, and yesterday I lost one just over four feet long."

"What bad luck," Nick said. "I hate losing a big fish once I've *hooked* him."

"Who's talking about fish?" the farmer said. "It's two of my kids that I lost!"

尼克很兴奋，所有钓鱼的人都想钓到真正的大鱼。

"有多大？"他问。

"嗯，"农民告诉他，"上周我失去了一个三英尺长的，昨天我失去了一个四英尺长的。"

"太不幸了。"尼克说，"我讨厌失去上钩的鱼。"

"谁说鱼了？"农民说，"我失去的是我的两个孩子。"。

---

lose *v.* 失去；错过   hook *v.* 钩住

22

Dog for Sale

Aman walked into a *pet* shop one day with a large and very ugly dog. It had long hair, short legs, no tail and a very wet nose.

"Good morning sir," the owner of the pet shop said. "How can I help you?"

"I want to sell this dog."

The pet shop owner looked at the dog and shook his head.

卖狗

一天，一个人牵着一只又大又丑的狗走进一家宠物商店。这条狗毛很长，腿很短，没有尾巴，还有一只湿湿的鼻子。

"早上好，先生，"宠物店老板说。"有什么可以帮忙的吗？"

"我想把这只狗卖掉。"

老板看了看这只狗，摇了摇头。

---

pet *n.* 宠物

"I'm sorry. I can't give you anything for that animal. No one will want to buy him."

"Why not?" asked the man. "He's clean, well-behaved and *healthy*."

"Look at him sir," said the pet shop owner. "He hasn't got a tail, his legs are too short and his hair's too long. Who would want to buy such a dog?"

"Well, I guess you're right," the man said. "But he can talk."

"What do you mean he can talk?" the pet shop owner asked.

"Yes, he can speak perfect English. Just listen," the man answered.

The dog then spoke.

"It's true sir," he said. "I am the world's greatest talking dog. I've been to the United States and talked to the President at the White

---

"对不起，这个家伙一分钱也卖不了，没人愿意买的。"

"为什么没有人愿意买呢？" 这个人问，"他爱干净、懂礼貌，而且很健康。"

"看看它吧，先生，" 宠物店老板说，"它没尾巴，腿太短，毛太长，谁能想买这样一只狗呢？"

"你可能是对的。"男人说。"但是它会说话。"

"你说它会说话，什么意思？" 老板问。

"它能讲一口漂亮的英语。"男人回答。

狗开始说话了。"真的，先生，"他说，"我是世界上最伟大的会说

---

healthy *adj.* 健康的

House in Washington. I've talked to the *Queen* of England and the *Emperor* of Japan. Please buy me sir; this man is very *cruel* to me. He makes me work too hard and doesn't feed me very well. He never takes me for a walk or gives me a bath. Sometimes he leaves me alone for weeks. I'm so unhappy sir. Please buy me and find a good home for me."

The pet shop owner could hardly believe what he was hearing.

"That's *amazing*," he said. "You're right. He is a talking dog. But tell me, why do you want to sell him?"

"Because I'm tired of all his lies," the man said.

话的狗。我去过美国，在华盛顿白宫与总统谈过话。我也与英国女皇、日本天皇聊过天。先生，买我吧；这个人对我太残忍。他总让我努力工作，还不好好给我喂食。他从不带我散步，给我洗澡，有时他好几个星期都不管我。先生，我很难过。买下我吧，为我找一个好的主人。"

宠物店老板简直不敢相信自己听到的话。

"太神奇了。"他说，"你是对的，它的确是一只会说话的狗，但请告诉我，你为什么要卖掉它呢？"

"因为我已经厌倦了它所有的谎言。"男人说。

---

queen *n.* 女王

cruel *adj.* 残忍的；残酷的

emperor *n.* 皇帝

amazing *adj.* 令人吃惊的

23

Breaking the News

A very old lady won a million dollars in a *lottery*. Her son and his wife heard the news on the radio.

"How are we going to tell your mother?" the wife asked. "The *shock* might kill her!"

"That's true," the son said. "Perhaps we'd better speak to her

---

透露消息

一位老妇人中了一百万美元的彩票大奖，她的儿子、儿媳在广播中听到了这个消息。

"我们怎样告诉你妈妈这个消息呢？"妻子问，"这么轰动的消息也许会害死她。"

"对啊，"儿子说，"也许我们该找她的医生谈谈，他能知道如何把这个消息慢慢地透露给她。"

---

lottery *n.* 彩票；抽奖　　　　　　　　shock *n.* 震惊；令人震惊的事

doctor about it. He'll know how to break the news to her *gently*."

They explained the situation to the old lady's doctor.

"I'm glad you told me," he said. "A shock, even a happy one, could give her a *heart attack*. Leave it to me. I'll find a way of breaking the news to her."

He thought about the problem for several days, and finally decided what he would say.

He called on the old lady and sat by her bedside. He took her hand in his.

"Let's play a game, my dear," he said. "A 'Let's *Pretend*' game."

"Oh, yes," the old lady said. "I love 'Let's Pretend' games."

"Good. I'll ask you a question first," the doctor said. "Then you

---

他们把情况告诉了老妇人的医生。

"我很高兴你们能告诉我。"医生说，"即使是好的震惊，也会使她犯心脏病的。交给我吧，我会找到把消息透露给她的方法。"

他想了好几天，最后想出了一个好办法。

他拜访了老妇人，并坐在她旁边。把她的手放在自己的手中。

"亲爱的，我们做个游戏。"他说，"一种'让我们假设'的游戏。"

"好，"老妇人说，"我喜欢'让我们假设'的游戏。"

"好，我先问你一个问题，"医生说。"然后你再问我一个。"

---

gently *adv.* 轻轻地；温柔地
heart attack 心脏病；心力衰竭

pretend *v.* 假装；装作

can ask me one."

He pretended to think for a few moments. Then he said, "Tell me, what would you do if you won a million dollars in the lottery?"

"Oh, that's an easy one," the old lady said. "I'd give most of it to you, doctor, because you have been so good to me all these years. Doctor!"

But the doctor was now lying on the floor. He had died of shock.

他假装想了一会，说"告诉我，假设你买彩票中了一百万美元你会做什么？"

"噢，很简单，"老妇人说，"我会把大多数的钱都给你，因为这些年你对我这么好，我的医生！"

老妇人话音一落，医生就倒在了地板上，他激动得心脏病突发过世了。

24

A Mailman's Problem

Charles was a mailman.

Six days a week he rode his bicycle from village to *village delivering* letters. He knew everybody and everybody knew him.

"Here comes Charles," the children called, and their parents came to the doors of their houses. Everybody liked Charles, and of course everyone especially liked

---

一位邮递员的疑问

查理是一位邮递员。

每周有六天他都要骑自行车往来各乡镇送信。他跟大家都很熟。

"查理来了！"孩子们喊道，然后他们父母就会来到房门口。每个人都很喜欢查理，当然，更喜欢得到他送来的信。

---

village *n.* 乡村；村庄

deliver *v.* 投递；传送

getting letters.

"Something for you today," Charles would call, and he would get off his bicycle and take a letter or a package out of the bag.

Or he would say, "Sorry, nothing for you today," and ride on.

Even the dogs knew and liked Charles, and although they *barked* at strangers, they never barked at him.

Except for one dog. Its owner, Mrs Taylor, had not lived in the village for very long, and every time the dog saw Charles, it started barking.

When he came to Mrs Taylor's house, Charles rode his bicycle faster. There were never any letters for her, so he did not have to stop.

"今天有你的东西！"查理会这样说，然后跳下自行车，从包里拿出信或包裹。

或者他会说，"对不起，今天没有你的邮件。"然后骑车继续走。

尽管狗总是会冲陌生人狂吠，但从来不冲查理叫，因为狗也认识并喜欢查理。

村庄住着一位泰勒夫人，她养了一只狗；因为她们来这里居住的时间并不长，所以这只狗每次见到查理都会叫。

每次查理都会飞快地穿过泰勒夫人家，因为从来没有她的信，所以他没必要停下来。

---

bark *v.* （狗）吠；叫

Then one day, there was a letter for her. Charles stopped his bicycle some way from Mrs Taylor's house. The dog started barking. Mrs Taylor came to the door.

"A letter for you!" Charles shouted.

"Why can't you bring it to me?" Mrs Taylor shouted back.

"What about your dog?" Charles said. "I don't want it to bite me."

Mrs Taylor laughed. "Don't be *frightened*," she said. "Everyone knows the old *saying*: A barking dog never bites."

"You know the old saying, and I know the old saying," Charles said, "but how do we know that your dog knows it?"

一天，有一封给泰勒夫人的信，查理在离她家不远的地方停了下来，这时狗就开始叫，泰勒夫人来到门口。

"你的信！"查理喊。

"你为什么不把它拿给我呢？"泰勒夫人大声问。

"你的狗啊，"查理说，"我不想让它咬我。"

泰勒夫人笑着说，"别害怕。"她说。"人人都知道一句古老的谚语：会叫的狗不咬人。"

"你知道这句谚语，我也知道！"查理说。"但是我们怎么知道你的狗也知道呢？"

---

frightened *adj.* 恐惧的；害怕的　　　　　　　　saying *n.* 谚语；俗语

25

Up, Not Out

Mark and Tim were working at a construction site. They were helping to build a very large *skyscraper*.

Their job was to pick up all the *garbage*, put it in *wheelbarrows* and take it to the garbage cans.

It was not difficult work, but it was a little dangerous. They had to walk beneath

向上看

马克和蒂姆在一个建筑工地工作，他们忙着建一座摩天大楼。

他们的工作是捡工地上的垃圾：把垃圾拾到手推车里，然后倒入垃圾箱。

这个工作并不难，只是有一点危险。他们必须经过工人们干活的地方。有时，工人们的工具会从离地几十英尺的摩天大楼顶层掉到地上。

---

skyscraper *n.* 摩天大楼   garbage *n.* 垃圾
wheelbarrow *n.* 独轮手推车

where men were working. Sometimes these men dropped their *tools* from the top of the skyscraper to the ground many feet below.

One morning, Mark was pushing his wheelbarrow toward the garbage cans when a voice shouted, "Look out!"

But Mark did not "look out". He looked up. And as he did so, a saw fell from the top of the skyscraper.

As it passed Mark's head, the saw cut off one of his ears.

Immediately he put his hand to his ear and cried out, "I've lost an ear. Help! Help!"

Tim ran up to help his friend.

"Look for my ear," Mark told him. "It's on the ground somewhere."

While Mark held a *handkerchief* to his head to stop the *bleeding*,

---

一天早晨，马克正把车推向垃圾箱，听到有人喊，"当心！(look out)"

但他没有"向外看(look out)"，抬头向上看。这时，一个大锯从大楼顶层掉下来。

锯经过马克头部，割掉了他的一只耳朵。

他赶快用手捂住耳朵，喊道，"我失去了一只耳朵，救命啊！救命啊！"

蒂姆跑来帮忙。

"快找我的耳朵。"马克告诉他，"掉在地上了。"

当马克拿手绢给耳朵止血时，蒂姆到处找耳朵。

---

tool *n.* 工具   handkerchief *n.* 手帕
bleeding *n.* 流血；失血

Tim looked everywhere for the missing ear.

At last he found an ear on the ground. He picked it up and carried it to Mark.

"Here you are," he said. "I've found it."

Mark looked at it. "No, that's not my ear," he said. "Mine had a *cigarette* behind it."

最后他找到了一只耳朵，捡起来交给马克。

"给你，"他说，"找到了。"

马克看了看这只耳朵，"不，那不是我的耳朵，"他说。"我的耳朵后面别了一支烟。"

---

cigarette *n.* 香烟；纸烟

More Uses Than One

Right after Zach's wedding, his wife's mother came to live with them.

She was not an easy woman to live with. She was always complaining and never seemed to stop talking.

Zach loved his wife but her mother was making his life *miserable*.

温度计的妙用

扎克结婚后，岳母便搬来和他们一起住。

她并不是一个容易相处的女人，总是抱怨，而且一刻不停地唠叨。

扎克爱妻子，但岳母把他的生活搅得痛苦不堪。

miserable *adj.* 痛苦的；悲惨的

Unfortunately, his wife would not listen to any *criticism* of her mother.

"She is my mother," she said. "I must *respect* her and so must you."

As the months passed, Zach became more and more unhappy. If only, he thought, there was some way of stopping his mother-in-law from talking all the time.

Then one day she was ill. She complained, of course. She was hot. She was cold. Her legs ached. Her head ached. She couldn't eat. She couldn't sleep.

At last, Zach sent for the doctor.

The doctor arrived. He examined her and then put a *thermometer* in her mouth. He wanted to take her *temperature*. "Sit quietly," he

不幸的是，他妻子从来听不进去任何批评她妈妈的话。

"她是我妈妈，"她说。"我必须尊重她，你也一样。"

数月以后，扎克越来越不开心。他想，只能想个办法阻止岳母唠叨不停。

一天，岳母生病了。当然，她又抱怨了——时冷时热、腿疼、头痛，不能吃也不能睡。

最后，扎克找来了医生。

医生到了，给她检查了身体，然后把体温计放进她嘴里。想测一测

criticism *n.* 指责；批评 respect *v.* 尊敬（某人）；尊重
thermometer *n.* 体温计 temperature *n.* 温度

said, "and don't open your mouth." Zach watched with surprise as his mother-in-law lay in bed with the thermometer in her mouth and her mouth closed.

For the first time since his wedding, he could not hear his mother-in-law's voice.

He walked up to the doctor, pointed at the thermometer and *whispered* in the doctor's ear. "How much do you want for that thing?"

体温。"安静坐好,"他说,"别张嘴。" 扎克惊喜地看到岳母躺在床上,嘴里叼着体温计,嘴闭得严严的。

自结婚以来,他第一次没听见岳母说话。

他走近医生,指着温度计,在医生耳边轻声说:"那个东西你要多少钱?"

---

whisper *v.* 低声说;耳语

27

An Unexpected Hobby

Jody lived in the country, but one year she decided to visit the *capital* city to do some shopping and to see the *sights*.

She stayed at a hotel near the central market. She had seldom been to the city before, and was very excited about what she would find.

On the first morning of her visit, as she walked from the hotel to

---

意想不到的爱好

乔迪住在乡下，有一年她决定到首都去购物、观光。

她在中央市场附近的宾馆住下。之前她从来没来过这座城市，因此她对看到的一切都感到异常兴奋。

来到城市的第一个早晨，从宾馆到市场的路上，她遇到了一个乞丐。

---

capital *n.* 首都

sight *n.* 景象；视野

the market, she passed a *beggar*.

He was holding up a notice which said, "Blind from birth. Please give generously."

Jody felt sorry for the blind beggar, and she *bent* down and put a dollar coin into his bowl.

"Thank you," he said.

On the second day, Jody passed the blind beggar again, and she gave him another dollar.

On the third day, however, Jody did not have a dollar coin. She had only fifty cents, so she dropped this into the beggar's bowl.

"What have I done wrong?" the beggar said. "Why are you so *stingy* today?"

乞丐手里拿着告示，写着"天生失明，行行好吧。"

乔迪很同情这个失明的乞丐，她弯下腰往乞丐的碗里放了一个一美元的硬币。

"谢谢。"他说。

第二天，乔迪又一次路过失明的乞丐身边，又给了他一美元。

但第三天，乔迪没有一美元的硬币，只有50分的硬币。于是她把硬币扔进了乞丐的碗里。

"我做错什么了？"乞丐说，"你今天怎么这么小气？"

---

beggar *n.* 乞丐　　　　　　　　　　　　　　　　　　bend *n.* 弯腰
stingy *adj.* 小气的；吝啬的

Jody was very surprised by what the beggar said.

"How do you know I haven't given you a dollar?" she said. "If you're blind, you can't know what coin I put into your bowl."

"Ah," explained the beggar, "the truth is I'm not blind. I'm just looking after this place for the regular beggar while he's on vacation."

"On vacation!" Jody *exclaimed*. "And what exactly does your blind friend do on vacation?"

"He goes into the country," the man said, "and takes pictures. He's a very good *photographer*."

乔迪被乞丐的话吓了一跳。

"你怎么知道我没给你一美元？"她说，"既然你看不见，你怎么会知道我放的是什么硬币啊？"

"嗯，"乞丐解释说，"事实上我不是盲人，这里的乞丐去度假了，我只是过来照看这个地方的。"

"度假！"乔迪惊叹道，"你那失明的朋友假期能做什么啊？"

"他去乡下，"那人说，"拍照片，他是个很好的摄影师。"

---

exclaim v. 呼喊；大叫

photographer n. 摄影师；摄影家

28

Three Wishes

Three *explorers*, an Englishman, an American and an Australian, were lost in the *jungle*. They had left home six months earlier to explore the jungle and gotten lost.

They had no food left, and they were weak and ill. They knew that if they did not find a village soon, they would die.

三个愿望

有三个探险家，一个英国人，一个美国人，一个澳大利亚人，他们在丛林里迷路了。他们是六个月之前到丛林探险的。

他们没有食物，身体也很虚弱，还生病了。他们知道如果不尽快找到一个村庄的话，他们就会死掉。

---

explorer *n.* 探险者；考察者   jungle *n.* 丛林；密林

Then, during the night, they were visited by a jungle *spirit*.

"I am the spirit of the jungle," it said. "I feel sorry for you. You may have three wishes."

"Does that mean three wishes each, or three wishes total?" the American explorer asked.

"I will give each of you one wish," the spirit of the jungle said.

The English explorer, who was very polite, said to the American and Australian explorers, "Please, you wish first."

The Australian explorer, who was just as polite as the Englishman, said, "Please, you wish first."

"Very well," the Englishman said. "I don't have to think for a minute. I know exactly what to wish for. I wish to be back home with my wife and family."

夜里，丛林里的一个精灵来看望他们。

"我是丛林里的精灵，"它说，"我替你们感到难过。你们可以许三个愿望。"

"是每个人三个愿望，还是一共三个愿望？"美国探险家问。

"我允许你们每个人许一个愿望。"精灵说。

英国探险家很有礼貌地跟美国探险家和澳大利亚探险家说，"你们先许愿吧。"

和英国人一样有礼貌的澳大利亚人说，"你们先许愿吧！"

"好吧，"英国人说，"我不用思索。我知道许什么愿，我希望回家

---

spirit *n.* 超自然的生物（精灵、仙子等）

Immediately he *disappeared*.

"That's wonderful," the Australian explorer said. "My wish is similar. I'd like to be back in Australia."

And immediately he disappeared. The American was left alone.

"And what is your wish?" the spirit of the jungle asked him.

"Those two explorers were nice men," the American explorer said. "We became close friends. To tell you the truth, I am feeling rather lonely here without them. I wish they were back here again."

和家人团圆。"

他马上消失了。

"太好了，"澳大利亚人说，"我的愿望也差不多，我希望回到澳大利亚。"

他马上消失了，只剩下美国人了。

"你的愿望是什么？"精灵问他。

"这两个探险家是个好人，"美国人说，"我们成了很要好的朋友，说实话，没有他们我感到很孤独，我希望他们能够回来。"

---

disappear *v.* 消失；不见

A Pain in the Neck

For many years Eric Miller worked on a farm, but then an uncle died and left him his business in the city.

Eric left the farm and went to work in the city. For the first time in his life he dressed like a *businessman*. His uncle had been about the same size, so Eric wore his clothes.

疼痛的脖子

埃里克·米勒在农场工作了很多年，但是叔叔死后，把城里的产业留给了他。

埃里克离开农场去城里工作。他平生第一次穿得像个商人。他身材和叔叔相同，因此，埃里克穿上了叔叔的衣服。

businessman *n.* 商人

But city life was not good for Eric, because after a few days he began to get very bad pains in his *neck*. He had never had pains in his neck before, and he was quite worried.

Each day the pains got worse. Finally he went to a doctor.

He undressed and the doctor examined him.

When the examination was over, the doctor told him to sit down.

"I've got very bad news for you," he said. "You've only got six months to live. Have a good time. Enjoy yourself while you can."

Eric took the doctor's advice. He sold his uncle's business and decided to travel around the world.

But first he wanted to buy himself some nice clothes. He went to the most expensive *tailor* in the city. "I'd like a *dozen* of your best

---

但是城市的生活并不适合他，过了几天，脖子就开始痛。他之前从来不这样，因此他非常担心。

疼痛每天都会加重，最后他去看医生。

他脱掉衣服，医生给他检查身体。

检查结束后，医生让他坐下。

"我有个坏消息告诉你，"他说，"你只有六个月的生命了，希望你过得愉快，尽可能地享受吧！"

埃里克接受了医生的建议。他变卖了叔叔的产业，决定环游世界。

但首先他想给自己买些好衣服。于是他找到城里最昂贵的裁缝。"我

---

neck *n.* 脖子
dozen *n.* 一打；十二个

tailor *n.* 裁缝

shirts," he said.

"Certainly, sir. I'll take your *measurements*."

The tailor measured Eric and wrote down the measurements. Eric saw that he had written down a size 16 neck.

"You've made a mistake," he told him. "My neck size is 14. All my shirts are *size* 14."

"No sir," the tailor said. "You may be wearing a size 14, but your neck is a size 16. And if you continue to wear a size 14, sooner or later you'll get very bad pains in your neck."

想要一打你这里最好的衬衫。"他说。

"当然，先生。我给你量量尺寸。"

裁缝量好尺寸并记了下来。埃里克看到裁缝已经记下了他衣领的尺寸：16。

"你犯了个错误，"他告诉他，"我衣领尺寸是14，我所有的衬衫都应该是14的。"

"不，先生，"裁缝说，"你可以穿14的，但你脖子是16的。如果你继续穿14的，脖子迟早会疼的。"

---

measurement *n.* 测量；尺寸   size *n.* 大小；尺寸

A Safe Bet

It was after seven in the afternoon when a man walked into a bar, ordered a drink and turned to watch the television.

The seven o'clock news was on and there was a film showing a man standing on top of a tall building. He was looking down at the crowd of people below.

一个安全的赌注

晚上7点多，一个男人走进酒吧，点了一杯酒，然后转身去看电视。

电视上正在播7点新闻，画面上有个人站在高楼顶上，正看着下面的人群。

On the ground, a police officer with a *megaphone* was trying to *persuade* him not to jump.

"Let's talk about your problem," the police officer was saying. "Perhaps we can help you."

The man in the bar turned to the bartender and said, "I bet you a hundred dollars he doesn't jump."

The bartender looked at him. "You're offering me a hundred dollars if he jumps? Is that right?"

"Yes. I don't think he'll jump."

The bartender smiled. "OK. You've got a bet."

The man turned back to the television set and watched it carefully. The bartender, however, did not seem to be very interested. He filled the man's glass and continued serving the other customers.

地面上，一个警察拿着扩音器试图劝他不要跳下来。

"让我们谈谈你的问题，"警察说，"也许我们能帮你。"

这个男人对酒保说，"我跟你赌100美元他不会跳。"

酒保看看他，"如果他跳了你给我100美元？对吗？"

"是的，我认为他不会跳。"

酒保笑着说，"好，我跟你赌。"

男人回到电视机前继续认真看电视。但酒保似乎并不感兴趣。他把男人的酒杯倒满酒，继续招呼其他客人。

---

megaphone *n.* 喇叭筒；扩音器

persuade *n.* 劝说；说服

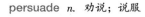

Then, after about five minutes, the man on the building threw himself off the roof and fell to the ground. The man in the bar turned to the bartender.

"He jumped," he said. "You win."

He held out a hundred-dollar *bill* to the bartender, but the bartender would not take it. "I can't take your money," he said. "I knew I couldn't lose. That story was on the six o'clock news. I saw him jump."

"Well, yes, so did I," the man said, "but I didn't think he'd do such a stupid thing twice."

大约5分钟后，楼顶上的人跳了下来，落在了地上。酒吧里的男人转向酒保。

"他跳了，"他说，"你赢了。"

他拿出了100美元的钞票交给酒保。但是酒保没拿。"我不能要你的钱，"他说。"我知道我不会输。这件事在6点新闻就报道过。我看见他跳的。"

"噢，我也看过，"男人说，"但是我没想到他会再次做这么愚蠢的事。"

---

bill *n.* 钞票

31

Flying the Flag

Steven and Frank wanted to be *heroes*.

"I want people to read about us in the history books," Steven said. "I want to do something that will be remembered forever."

"Me too," Frank said. "But what can we do?"

放飞旗帜

史蒂文和富兰克想成为英雄。

"我希望人们在历史书上能读到关于我们的事迹，"史蒂文说，"我要做一些永远被别人记住的事。"

"我也是。"富兰克说，"但我们怎么做呢？"

---

hero *n.* 英雄

The two men thought about this for many weeks, and then Steven said, "Let's climb the highest mountain in the world. Then we'll be remembered."

"That's a good idea," Frank said, "but how can we prove that we have climbed it?"

"We'll put a *flag* on the top," Steven said. "Anyone flying over the mountain in an airplane will see it."

Frank agreed that this was a good idea, and the two men set off.

They walked for three weeks to reach the bottom of the mountain, and then they began to climb.

The mountain was very *steep* and they could climb only a few hundred feet a day. At night they slept in a small *tent*.

两个人想了好几周，然后史蒂文说，"咱们攀登世界上最高的山峰吧。那样我们将会被永远铭记。"

"好主意，"富兰克说。"但是怎样证明我们攀登过最高山峰呢？"

"我们在山顶上插一面旗帜，"史蒂文说，"每一个坐飞机飞过山顶的人都会看见它。"

富兰克也认为这是个好主意，于是两个人出发了。

他们走了三周才到达山脚，然后开始攀登。

山很陡，他们一天只能爬几百英尺。夜晚，他们睡在小帐篷里。

---

flag *n.* 旗；旗帜

tent *n.* 帐篷

steep *adj.* 陡峭的；险峻的

It was very cold on the mountain and soon they were climbing across snow and ice. But at last, after many days of *hardship*, they reached the top.

"We've made it, Steven," Frank said. "We've finally climbed to the top of the highest mountain in the world. We'll be famous. All we have to do now is plant our flag in the ice."

"That's right," Steven said, "and then we can go home."

He waited for Frank to plant the flag. When Frank did nothing, Steven said, "Why aren't you planting the flag?"

"I don't have it," Frank said. "I thought you had it."

山上很冷，很快就变成在冰雪上行进了。但最后，经过很多天的努力，终于到达了山顶。

"我们成功了，史蒂文，"富兰克说，"我们终于攀登了世界最高的山峰，我们出名了。现在要做的是把旗插在冰里。"

"对，"史蒂文说，"然后再回家。"

他等着富兰克插旗。可富兰克什么也没做，史蒂文说，"为什么不插旗啊？"

"我没有旗啊，"富兰克说，"我以为你有呢！"

---

hardship *n.* 艰苦；困苦

32

Safe Hands

A *fire engine* raced through the streets to a fire. Its *siren* was screaming "Wee-ooo, wee-ooo, wee-ooo."

It was not long before the engine reached the fire. Smoke was *pouring* out of an apartment building where many people lived. There were flames coming out of the top-floor windows.

The firemen quickly connected their *hoses* and began to pour

安全的手

消防车正飞奔着要去救火，警报器一直在响："呜呜……呜呜……呜呜……"。

不一会儿，消防车来到了火灾现场。浓烟从一栋住了很多人的公寓里滚滚而出。顶楼的窗户里也窜出了火花。

消防员赶紧接好水带，开始向大楼浇水灭火。

---

fire engine 救火车；消防车
pour *v.* 倒；灌

siren *n.* 汽笛；警报
hose *n.* 橡皮软管；塑料软管

water onto the building.

Then a woman appeared in one of the top-floor windows.

"Help!" she cried. "Help!"

She had a small baby in her arms.

"Throw the baby down," one of the firemen called. He was a big strong man with wide shoulders.

"I don't dare," the woman shouted. "You might drop him."

The fireman laughed.

"Don't worry," he said. "I won't drop him. I'm the *goalkeeper* for the fire department's soccer team."

The woman looked down at the fireman. She saw his wide shoulders and big hands.

一个女人出现在顶楼的一个窗户前。

"救命啊！"她喊道。"救命啊！"

她怀里还抱着个婴儿。

"把孩子扔下来，"一个消防员喊。他身材高大，体格强壮，肩膀也很宽阔。

"我不敢，"女人喊道，"你可能接不住。"

消防员笑了。

"别担心。"他说，"我不会让他摔到的，我是消防足球队的守门员。"

女人向下看了看，看到了消防员宽宽的肩膀和一双大手。

---

goalkeeper *n.* 守门员

"All right," she said.

She leaned out of the window and dropped the baby. It fell safely into the fireman's hands, just like a soccer ball, and for a moment he forgot where he was and what he was doing.

He *bounced* the baby three times and then *kicked* it halfway up the street.

"好。"她说。

她倚向窗外，把孩子扔了下去。孩子安全地落到消防员手中，就像一个足球一样。一时间，消防员忘了自己在哪，正在做什么。

他把孩子扔起了三次，然后高高踢起，孩子落在了街中央。

---

bounce *v.* 反跳；弹起   kick *v.* 踢

33

A Voice from Heaven

Mrs Lopez and her mother lived together in the United States. Mrs Lopez had been there many years, but her mother had only recently arrived from Mexico. After just two months, Mrs Lopez's mother died. Mrs Lopez was very unhappy. She loved her mother very much and missed her.

One day, Mrs Lopez was walking

天堂之音

洛佩兹小姐和她妈妈一起住在美国，她已经在那里住了很多年了。但她妈妈最近才从墨西哥来到这里。两个月后，妈妈去世了。洛佩兹小姐很伤心。她非常爱妈妈，也很想她。

一天，洛佩兹小姐正走在大街上，忽然，她看见一间公寓外贴了一则通知。

along the street when she saw a notice outside an apartment building.

The notice said, "Madame Rita, *Spiritual Medium*. Room 454. Fourth floor. I can help you contact your *departed* loved ones."

Mrs Lopez thought, "I'd like to ask my mother how she is. Perhaps I should visit this Madame Rita."

She went into the building and took the elevator to the fourth floor. She soon found Room 454 and went inside.

Madame Rita said, "How can I help you?"

"I want to speak to my mother. She died last year."

"What was her name?" Madame Rita asked.

"Carla," Mrs Lopez said.

通知写着，"丽塔女士，精神传媒。454室，4楼。我可以帮你联系逝去的爱人。"

洛佩兹想，"我想问问妈妈现在怎么样了，也许我应该拜访这位丽塔女士。"

她走进公寓乘电梯到了四楼，很快找到了454室，然后走了进去。

丽塔女士说，"有什么需要帮忙的吗？"

"我想和妈妈说话，她去年去世的。"

"她叫什么名字？"丽塔女士问。

"卡拉，"洛佩兹小姐说。

---

spiritual *adj.* 精神的；心灵的   medium *n.* 媒介；方法
departed *adj.* 过去的；死去的

"I can help you," Madame Rita said. "It will cost $200."

"All right," Mrs Lopez said.

Madame Rita closed her eyes. She was silent for several minutes. Then she spoke.

"Carla, can you hear me?" she said.

A voice came out of nowhere. "Yes, I can hear you."

"Your daughter wants to know if you are happy."

"Yes, I am very happy," the voice said.

Madame Rita opened her eyes. "Did you hear what your mother said?" she asked Mrs Lopez.

"Yes," Mrs Lopez said.

"我可以帮助你，"瑞塔女士说，"不过得花200美元。"

"好，"洛佩兹小姐说。

丽塔女士闭上眼睛，沉默了几分钟后开始讲话。

"卡拉，你能听见我说话吗？"她问。

一个声音不知道从哪里传出来，"是的，我能听见。"

"女儿想知道你是否快乐。"

"是的，我很快乐。"那个声音说。

丽塔睁开眼睛，"你听见妈妈说什么了吗？"她问洛佩兹小姐。

"是的。"洛佩兹小姐说。

"Then that will be two hundred dollars," Madame Rita said.

"Fine," Mrs Lopez said, "I will pay you if you can explain how my ninety-year-old mother learned to speak such good English. She couldn't speak it when she was *alive*."

"好，200美元。"瑞塔女士说。

"好，" 洛佩兹小姐说，"但如果你能解释我90岁的母亲为什么能说这么流利的英语，我就付钱。她生前是不会说英语的啊。"

---

alive *adj.* 活着的；在世的

34

Boasting

The British, rightly or wrongly, think that Americans are *boastful*, because the Unite States is a big country full of big things and Americans are proud of them.

On one occasion an American boy visited an English school as an *exchange* student. He was looked

after by Alec Wilson, one of the English boys at the school.

吹牛

不管对错，英国人都认为美国人很能吹牛，因为美国地大物博，美国人总为此感到自豪。

有一次，一个美国男孩作为交换学生到一所英国学校参观，得到了亚历克·威尔逊的照顾，亚历克是个男孩，是这所学校的学生。

---

boastful *adj.* 自夸的；吹嘘的　　　　　　　　on one occasion 有一次
exchange *n.* 交换；交流

Alec took him around London and showed him the sights.

"That's Buckingham Palace," he said, pointing to the building. "It's where the Queen lives, and it took three years to build."

"That's nothing," the American boy said. "The White House, where the President lives, is bigger than that and took only two years to build."

Later that morning, the two boys stood outside a large *church*.

"That's the most important church in London," Alec said, "Westminster Abbey. It took ten years to build."

"Back home," the American boy said, "Saint Patrick's Cathedral, which is much *grander* than that, took only nine years to build."

亚历克带他逛遍了伦敦，并给他介绍各处景点。

"那是白金汉宫"，他指着大楼说。"是女王住的地方，花了三年才建好。"

"那没什么，"美国男孩说，"总统住的白宫，比这个还要大，两年就建成了。"

随后的那个早上，两个男孩站在了一个大教堂外面。

"那是英国最重要的教堂，"亚历克说，"威斯敏斯特教堂，它耗用了十年时间建造的。"

"在美国，"美国男孩说，"圣派区克大教堂比这富丽堂皇，九年就建成了。"

---

church n. 教堂

grand adj. 壮丽的；壮观的

Next, Alec showed his American friend the huge Canary Wharf Tower. "That took three years to build," he said.

The American boy just laughed. "We've got lots of skyscrapers on Wall Street much higher than that," he said, "and they were built in half that time."

Finally, they came to the famous Tower Bridge. It was being opened to let a ship through.

The American boy was at last *impressed*. "What's that?" he demanded.

Alec decided to get his *revenge*.

"I don't know," he said. "It wasn't there this morning."

接着，亚历克向他的美国朋友介绍金丝雀码头大楼。"那座楼花了三年建成的，"他说。

美国男孩笑了笑说，"我们华尔街上有很多摩天大楼，比这高多了。"他说，"只花一年半就建好了。"

最后，他们来到了著名的塔桥，有条船正从桥下经过。

这让美国男孩很是钦佩。"那是什么？"他问。

亚历克决定报复一下他。

"我不知道，"他说，"今天早上还没在那儿呢！"

---

impressed *adj.* 有印象的   revenge *n.* 复仇；报复

A Large Farm

Texas is a huge state in the United States, and Texans often boast about how big everything is there.

One day a rich Texan *rancher* on vacation in Europe stopped at a house along the road. He had

been driving for many hours, the weather was hot, and he needed a

---

大农场

得克萨斯州是美国的一个大洲，那里的人经常吹嘘当地的东西如何之大。

一天，一个有钱的得克萨斯牧场主在欧洲度假，中途在临街的一座房子前停了下来。他已开了好几个小时的车了。天气很热，他很想来点清凉的饮料。

---

rancher *n.* 大牧场主；农场主

refreshing drink.

"I'm sorry to trouble you," he said to the man who answered the door, "but would it be *possible* for you to let me have a glass of water?"

The man looked his visitor up and down, as if to decide whether he could *trust* him or not. He finally said, "Of course," and invited the Texan to come into his house.

He poured the Texan a glass of cold water, and after drinking it, the Texan asked him, "Are you a farmer?"

"Yes," the man said. "I keep a few chickens."

"I'm also a farmer," the Texan said. "How big is your farm?"

"It's about a hundred meters by a hundred meters," the man said quite proudly. "What about your farm? How big is it?"

"很抱歉打扰你，"他对应门的人说，"可以给我一杯水吗？"

那个人打量了来访者，好像正在决定是否相信他。最后他说，"当然！"，然后他邀请这个得克萨斯牧场主进来。

他给牧场主倒了一杯凉水。喝完后，得克萨斯人问他，"你是农民吗？"

"是的，"那人说，"我养鸡。"

"我也是农民。"得克萨斯人说，"你的农场多大？"

"大概100平方米。"这个人骄傲地说。"你的农场呢？多大啊？"

---

refreshing *adj.* 凉爽的；提神的　　　　possible *adj.* 可能的
trust *v.* 信任；相信

"Well," the Texan said, "after I've had my breakfast, I get in my car and I drive and drive and drive. I keep on driving all day, and I don't reach the other side of my farm until dinner time."

The man looked at the Texan *sympathetically*. "Oh, I know how you feel," he said. "I once had a car like that."

"嗯，"得克萨斯人说，"用过早饭后，我开车，开啊开，开了一整天，到晚饭时也到不了另一边。"

那人同情地看着得克萨斯人。"噢，我知道你是什么感受了。"他说"我曾经也有一辆那样的车。"

---

sympathetically *adv.* 悲怜地，怜悯地；富有同情心地

36

Good News

When Susan Fisher left high school, she wanted to go to college. *Unfortunately*, her father was quite poor, and a university education cost a lot of money.

"Take the *entrance examination*", her father said, "and we'll think of something if you pass."

Susan took the examination. Her *score* wasn't very high, but it

好消息

苏珊·费舍尔高中毕业了，她想上大学。不幸的是，父亲太穷了，而上大学需要一大笔钱。

"参加大学入学考试吧，"父亲说："如果考上了，我们再想办法"。

苏珊参加了考试，分数不太高，但还可以，她被一所大学录取了。

unfortunately *adv.* 不幸地　　　　　　entrance examination 入学考试
score *n.* （在比赛或测试中）得分

was high enough, and she was offered a place at a university.

"I'm very proud of you, Susan," her father said. "I must find the money for a university education for you somehow."

"But how, Dad?" Susan asked.

"Well, I can sell my car and work a lot of *overtime*. I can even work two jobs if necessary, one during the day and one at night."

"You're a very *generous* father," Susan said.

"Your future is worth the *sacrifice*," he told her.

The next day, he sold his car and asked his boss to give him three hours of overtime every day. This meant walking to work and working 12 hours a day, seven days a week, but he did not *complain*. His daughter's education was worth it.

"我真为你自豪，苏姗，"父亲说："无论如何我也要筹到钱供你上学。"

"爸爸，怎么筹集呀？"苏姗问。

"这样吧，我把车子卖了，再加点班，如果有必要我可以打两份工：一份白班，一份夜班。"

"你真是太善良了，爸爸。"苏姗说。

"为了你的未来，我这点儿牺牲值得！"爸爸回答。

第二天，父亲卖了车子并向老板要求每天加班3小时——这就意味着他每天步行上班，工作12小时，每周工作7天。但他丝毫没有抱怨，为了

---

overtime *n.* 加班（时间）

sacrifice *n.* 牺牲

generous *adj.* 大方的；慷慨的

complain *v.* 发牢骚；抱怨

A year passed. Susan took her final exams.

When the results were *announced*, she ran home to tell her father the news. "Dad," she said, "I got my examination results. You'll be so pleased."

"You passed!" he exclaimed.

"No! You can have your car back and stop working so hard!"

女儿的教育——值得。

一年过去了，期末考试到了。

当老师宣布成绩后，苏姗飞奔着回家告诉父亲好消息："爸爸，考试成绩出来了，你看了会很高兴的。"

"你通过考试了！"爸爸惊喜地喊道。

"没有！你可以赎回车子，再也不用这么辛苦工作了！"苏姗说。

---

announce *v.* 宣布；宣告

37

Telling the Time

Wally worked in a shop that sold clocks. One day his next door neighbor, Harry, came into his shop. Harry was very *stingy*. His stinginess made Wally very angry.

Wally said to him, "When are you going to buy a clock?"

"Never," Harry said. "I don't need a clock."

报时

沃尔利在一家钟表店工作。一天，邻居亨利来到店里。亨利非常吝啬，这使得沃尔利十分生气。

沃尔利问："你打算什么时候买个钟啊？"

亨利回答说："永远不会买的，我也不需要钟啊。"

---

stingy *adj.* 小气的；吝啬的

"Everyone needs a clock," Wally said. "How do you know when it's time to get up?"

"The man who lives on the other side of me turns on his radio at seven o'clock for the news," Harry said. "I hear the *announcer* say, 'The time is seven o'clock. Here is the news.'"

"OK. But how do you know when to go to work?" Wally wanted to know.

"By the time I get out of bed, wash and *shave*, it's half past seven," Harry said. "By the time I've eaten my breakfast of toast, *jam* and coffee, it's eight o'clock, time to leave for the office. By the time I get to the bus stop, it's ten past eight. The bus arrives in a few minutes and by the time it gets to my stop, the time is half past eight. That's the time I start work."

沃尔利说："人人都需要钟表，要不你怎么知道什么时间起床呢？"

"我邻居每天七点钟时都会打开收音机收听新闻。"亨利回答："每天，我都会听到播音员说：'现在是七点钟，请听新闻报道。'"

"噢，是这样。那你又怎么知道何时上班呢？"沃尔利真的想知道。

"我每天起床、洗脸、刮胡子，这一切做完刚好七点半。"亨利说："当我吃完早饭——带果酱的吐司和一杯咖啡，刚好八点，这就该上班了。我用十分钟到公共汽车站，等几分钟车就来了，八点半准时到站，下车我就开始工作。"

---

announcer *n.* 播音员
jam *n.* 果酱

shave *v.* 刮（胡须、毛发）

"OK. But how do you know when it's time to go home?" Wally said, getting angry.

"The factory *siren* rings," Harry told him.

"How do you know when it's time to go to bed?"

"The television programs come to an end."

By now Wally was really angry. "OK," he shouted. "Now tell me what would happen if you woke up in the middle of the night and wanted to know the time?"

"That's easy," Harry said. "I've got a *hammer*."

"A hammer? What good is a hammer when you want to know the time?"

"I'd use it to knock on your wall. You'd shout at me, 'What are you doing knocking on my wall at three o'clock in the morning?'"

"好吧，那你又怎么知道什么时候下班呢？"沃尔利有些恼怒地问。

"工厂打下班铃啊！"

"那你又怎么知道什么时候上床睡觉呢？"

"电视节目播完了我就睡。"

这时，沃尔利真是气极了，他大声喊道："好吧，现在告诉我如果你半夜醒来想知道几点了，怎么办呢？"

"那还不容易？"亨利说："我有锤子啊。"

"一把锤子？锤子和时间有什么关系？"

"我就用它敲你的墙，你就会大声嚷嚷：'早晨三点钟你敲什么敲？'"。

---

siren *n.* 警报器；汽笛

hammer *n.* 铁锤；榔头

38

The World's Greatest Wonders

Three men traveling on a train began a conversation about the world's greatest wonders.

"In my opinion," the first man said, "*the Egyptian pyramids* are the world's greatest wonder. Although they were built thousands of years ago, they are still standing. And

---

世界上最伟大的奇迹

三个乘火车旅行的人在谈论世界上最伟大的奇迹。

第一个人说："我认为，埃及金字塔是世界上最伟大的奇迹。尽管建于数千年前，但它们至今仍矗立着，请记住：那时建金字塔的人只使用简单的工具。他们没有今天建筑工人和工程师使用的现代化工具。"

Egyptian *adj.* 埃及的；埃及人的   pyramid *n.* 金字塔

remember: the people who built them had only simple tools. They did not have the kind of *machinery* that builders and *engineers* have today."

"I agree that the pyramids in Egypt are wonderful," the second man said, "but I do not think they are the greatest wonder. I believe computers are more wonderful than the pyramids. They have taken people to the moon and brought them back safely. In seconds, they carry out *mathematical calculations* that would take a person a hundred years to do."

He turned to the third man and asked, "What do you think is the greatest wonder in the world?"

The third man thought for a long time, and then he said, "Well, I agree that the pyramids are wonderful, and I agree that computers

---

"金字塔的神奇是*毋庸置疑*的，"第二个人说："但我认为他还不是最神奇的。我相信计算机比金字塔要神奇得多，他们把人送上月球又把他们安全送回来。他们用几秒钟所做的数学运算够一个人算上100年！"

说着他转向第三个人问："你认为世界上最伟大的奇迹是什么？"

第三个人想了好长时间，然后说："好吧，我也认为金字塔和计算机同样神奇，但我认为最大的奇迹是保温瓶的发明。"

---

machinery *n.* 机器
mathematical *adj.* 数学的；关于数学的

engineer *n.* 工程师；机工
calculation *n.* 计算

are wonderful too. However, in my opinion, the most wonderful thing in the world is this *thermos*."

And he took a thermos out of his bag and held it up.

The other two men were very surprised. "A thermos?" they exclaimed. "But that's a simple thing."

"Oh, no, it's not," the third man said. "In the winter you put in a hot drink and it stays hot. In the summer you put in a cold drink and it stays cold. How does the thermos know whether it is winter or summer?"

他从兜子里掏出个保温瓶，举着说。

其他两个人十分吃惊："保温瓶？"他们惊叫道："这太简单了。"

"噢，不，一点也不简单，"第三个人说："在冬天，你把热饮装进去，它就保持温热；而夏天你把冷饮倒进去，它就保持凉爽。可保温瓶怎么就知道是冬天还是夏天呢？"

---

thermos *n.* 热水瓶；保温瓶

Friendly Advice

A movie *actor* went to visit a friend in another town. He walked around the town for a long time trying to find his friend's address, but he could not find it. Soon he got lost.

He decided to ask for directions. There was no one on the street, but he could see a shop on the corner. He walked towards it.

The shop was very small. It sold only newspapers and cigarettes.

友好的忠告

一个电影演员到另一个城市探望一个朋友。他在该城市转了很长时间也没有找到朋友的住址,很快就迷路了。

他决定问路,可街上空无一人。突然他看到街角有一家店铺,于是他走了过去。

店铺很小,只卖报纸和香烟。窗户玻璃上贴着一则告示,写着"铺面转让,入内咨询。"

---

actor *n.* 演员(尤指男演员)

In the window there was a *notice* that said, "Business For Sale. *Inquire* Within."

The movie actor went into the shop. There was an old man sitting behind the counter. He looked at the movie actor very carefully.

Then he said, "You're the man who's going to buy this shop."

The movie actor laughed. "No," he said. "I'm lost. Can you tell me how to get to Third Street?"

The old man stood up and walked to the door. He pointed down the street.

"Go down the street to the traffic light, and then turn right. Take the next left. Third Street is the first street on the right."

"Thank you very much," the actor said and walked away.

A few feet from the shop, he stopped walking. He was a very *vain*

　　电影演员走进店铺，柜台后面坐着一位老人，他上下仔细地审视了一番这位电影演员，然后问："你要买下这间铺子吧？"

　　这位电影演员笑着说，"不，我迷路了。你能告诉我第三大街怎么走吗？"

　　老人站起来走到门口，指向大街。

　　"沿着街向前走，到红绿灯处向右拐。再到路口时向左拐。右边的第一条街就是第三大街。"

　　"太谢谢了。"演员说完就走开了。

　　走了几步，他又停住了。他是个很自负的人，他想："这个老人如此

---

notice *n.* 公告　　　　　　　　　　　　　　　inquire *v.* 打听；询问
vain *adj.* 自负的；自视过高的

man, and he thought, "The old man looked at me very carefully. He knows who I am. Perhaps he wants my *autograph*."

He turned and walked back to the shop. The old man was still sitting behind the counter.

"You know who I am, don't you?" he said to him.

"Yeah," the old man said. "I told you. You're the man who's going to buy this shop."

"No, no," the movie actor said. "I'm a movie actor. Did you see my *last* movie?"

"Yeah, I saw it," the old man said. "And believe me, if you're *smart*, you will be the one to buy my shop."

细致地打量我，一定是认出我了，或许他想要我的亲笔签名呢。"

他又走回店铺。老人仍坐在柜台后。

"你知道我是谁，是吧？"他问。

"知道，"老人说："我知道，你就是要买下这个铺子的人。"

这位电影演员说："不，不，我是电影演员，你看过我最近拍的电影吗？"

老人答道："当然，我看了。相信我，如果你明智的话，就该买下我的店铺。"

---

autograph *n.* 亲笔签名
smart *adj.* 精明的；聪明的

last *adj.* 最近过去的；最新的

The Witch

"We should do something nice for the old people of our town," Miss Clark said to her class one day. "What can we do?"

"Can we give them a *picnic*?" one of the children asked. "We can send out *invitations* and bring cakes and *sausages* and all kinds of good things to eat."

"That's a very good idea," the teacher said. "We'll ask all the old

巫婆

一天，克拉克老师对班上的孩子们说："我们应该为镇上的老人做点好事，我们能做什么呢？"

"给他们提供一顿野餐怎么样？"一个孩子说："我们可以发出请帖，带上糕点、香肠和各种各样好吃的东西。"

老师说："好主意！我们邀请所有的老人到河边野餐吧。"

picnic *n.* 郊游；野餐   invitation *n.* 邀请；请帖
sausage *n.* 香肠

people to a picnic by the river."

The children worked hard getting ready for the picnic. Their parents made cakes and pies or gave money, and the children wrote invitation cards to the old people. Then they took the cards to the old people's homes.

On the morning of the picnic, the sky was blue and the sun was *shining*. The children were all *looking forward to* giving the old people a happy day.

Then one of the children said, "Oh, no! We forgot to invite Mrs Waller."

The children did not like Mrs Waller. She looked like a *witch*.

"Then we have to invite her now," the teacher said. "She will be hurt and angry if we don't ask her."

She looked around the class and then pointed at one of the boys.

孩子们十分用心地准备野餐，父母也帮他们烹制了蛋糕、馅饼，有的还给了钱。孩子们写好邀请卡，又把卡片送到老人家里。

到了野餐那天清晨，天空湛蓝、阳光普照，孩子们都盼着让老人们过上快乐的一天。

一个孩子突然说："噢！我们忘了邀请沃乐夫人。"

孩子们都不喜欢沃乐夫人——她看起来像个女巫。

"那只好现在邀请了，"老师说，"如果我们不邀请她，她会受到伤害而生气的。"

她看看全班同学，然后指着一名男生，说："汤姆，带上邀请卡去她

---

shine *v.* 发光；闪光
witch *n.* 女巫；巫婆

lood forward to 盼望；期待

"Tom, take an invitation card to her house. *Apologize* for being late. Don't tell her we forgot her."

Tom did not want to go to Mrs Waller's house, but he was a *brave* boy, and said, "All right, Miss Clark."

He went to the old woman's house and knocked on the door. Mrs Waller opened it. She looked very angry.

"Well," she said, "what is it? What do you want?"

Tom gave her the invitation card and said, "I'm sorry we did not ask you before, but please come to our picnic. It's a beautiful day."

Mrs Waller knew that the children thought she was a witch. She guessed that they had forgotten her.

"You're too late," the woman said. "It's a beautiful day now, but I've already arranged for rain this afternoon."

家吧。为迟到的邀请道歉，别告诉她我们把她忘了。"

虽然汤姆很不愿意去，但他是个勇敢的孩子，于是说："好吧，克拉克老师。"

他来到老妇人家，敲了敲门。沃乐夫人开了门，看起来气呼呼的。

"这是什么？你想干吗？"她说。

汤姆把邀请信给了她并说："太抱歉了，前几天没有邀请你。现在跟我们一起去野餐吧，今天的天气不错！"

沃乐夫人知道孩子们把她当女巫，她猜孩子们忘记邀请她了。

"你来晚了。"老妇人说："现在天气挺好，但下午我已经安排下雨了"。

---

apologize v. 道歉；认错

brave adj. 勇敢的；无所畏惧的

The Size of It

Ellen Parker was worried about her health. She could not walk very quickly and it was difficult for her to climb stairs. She was soon out of breath.

"I suppose I had better go to the doctor," she thought.

She went to the doctor and told him her problem.

"I'm not at all surprised," he said. "It's *obvious* what your problem is."

10磅肉有这么多

艾伦·帕克很担心自己的健康。她走路缓慢，上楼也很艰难，气喘吁吁。

"我想还是去看看医生吧。"她想。

她到医院，把自己的问题告诉了医生。

---

obvious *adj.* 明显的

He examined her and then gave her some advice.

"If you don't do what I say, Mrs Parker," he said, "then you will have a heart attack. It could kill you."

Ellen was very worried as she left the doctor's. She knew that she had to take his advice but that it would not be easy and that it would take time.

The next day she went shopping. The first shop she went into was a *butcher's* shop.

"I'd like ten pounds of steak please," she said.

"Certainly, madam," the butcher replied and went into the cold *storage room* and found a large piece of steak. He brought the huge piece of meat back into the shop and placed it on the *scale*.

医生说："我一点也不惊讶，你的问题太明显了。"

检查完毕，医生给了她几点忠告。

"如果你不按我说的去做，帕克夫人，你极有可能得心脏病，那可是致命的呀。"

艾伦忧心忡忡地走出医生办公室，她知道必须遵从医生的忠告，但这绝非易事，是需要时间的。

第二天她去购物，走进的第一家店铺是肉铺。

"请给我称10磅牛排。"她说

"好的，夫人，"肉贩回答。他走进冷冻室取出一大块牛排，然后回到铺子里把这一大块肉放在秤上。

---

butcher n. 屠户；卖肉的商贩
scale n. 磅秤；天平

storage room n. 储藏室

"That's just under ten pounds," he said.

"That's big enough," Mrs Parker said.

The butcher worked out the price.

"At 4 point 99 dollars a pound that will be 49 point 50 dollars, please. Would you like me to cut it up into smaller pieces for you?"

"Oh, I don't want to buy the meat," Mrs Parker said.

"If you don't want to buy it," the butcher replied angrily, "why did you ask me to get it for you?"

"My doctor told me that I am *overweight* and have to lose ten pounds. I wanted to see what ten pounds of *flesh* looked like."

"10磅还差一点，"肉贩说。

"够大了，"帕克夫人说。

肉贩算好了价钱。

"一磅肉4.99美元，一共49.50美元。用不用切成小块？"

"噢，我不想买肉，"帕克夫人说。

"如果你不想买，"肉贩气呼呼地说："为什么让我去取肉啊？"

"医生说我超重，必须减掉10磅肉。我想看看10磅肉到底有多少。"

---

overweight *adj.* 超重的   flesh *n.* 肉；肌肉

42

A Letter Home

Sarah Williams went to a *boarding school*. One day, her parents got a letter from her.

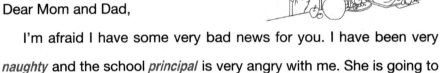

Wentworth Girls' School.

Shadyside. May 25th.

Dear Mom and Dad,

I'm afraid I have some very bad news for you. I have been very *naughty* and the school *principal* is very angry with me. She is going to

---

一封家书

莎拉·威廉姆斯在寄宿学校上学。一天，父母收到了她的一封信。

温特渥女子学校

林荫路

5月25日

亲爱的爸爸、妈妈：

恐怕我得告诉你们一个坏消息。由于我十分淘气，校长非常生气，她

---

boarding school 寄宿学校　　　　naughty *adj.* 不听话的；顽皮的
principal *n.* 校长；院长

write to you. You must come and take me away from here. She does not want me in the school any longer.

The trouble started last night when I was smoking a cigarette in bed. This is *against* the rules of course. We are not supposed to smoke at all.

As I was smoking, I heard *footsteps* coming towards the room. I did not want a teacher to catch me smoking, so I threw the cigarette away.

Unfortunately, the cigarette fell into the *wastebasket*, which caught fire.

There was a *curtain* near the wastebasket, which caught fire too. Soon the whole room was burning.

要给你们写信，让你们把我接走。她再也不想让我待在学校了。

麻烦发生在昨天晚上，我在床上抽烟——当然，这是违反校规的，我们是不可以抽烟的。

当我正抽烟时，走廊里传来了脚步声。我当然不希望被老师抓住，所以把烟丢掉了。

不幸的是，烟被我丢入了废纸篓，一下子着起火来。

挨着纸篓的窗帘也着火了，很快整个房间都着火了。

---

against *prep.* 违反；反对　　　　　　　footstep *n.* 脚步声
wastebasket *n.* 废纸篓　　　　　　　　curtain *n.* 窗帘；门帘

The principal phoned the fire department. The school is a long way from the town, and by the time the fire department arrived, the whole school was in flames. Many of the girls are in the hospital.

The principal says that the fire was all my fault and you must pay for the *damage*. She will send you a bill for about a million dollars.

I'm very sorry about this.

Love,

Sarah

Postscript: None of the above is true, but I have failed my exams. I just want you to know how bad things could have been!

校长给消防队打电话。可学校离城镇太远了，等消防车来时，整个学校都烧着了，许多女生都进了医院。

校长说火灾是我引起的，要求你们必须赔偿损失。他会给你寄张100万美元的账单的。

为此我非常抱歉。

爱你们的莎拉

附言：以上纯属杜撰，但我考试没及格，我只想让你们知道什么才是最糟糕的事情。

---

damage *n.* 损失；损害　　　　　　　　postscript *n.* 附笔；附言

43

Revenge

J ames had a terrible toothache. It kept him awake all night. His *cheek* was *swollen* and it was difficult for him to eat or drink. Anything very hot or cold made the toothache worse. If James ate anything sweet, the pain was *unbearable*.

James did not want to take time off from work, so he tried to bear the pain. He took a *painkiller* every hour.

报复

詹姆斯牙疼得厉害，整夜无法入睡。不仅面部肿胀，连吃饭、喝水都成了问题。任何冷、热的东西都会加剧他的牙疼。如果詹姆斯吃甜食，疼痛将无法忍受。

詹姆斯不想耽误工作，所以尽力忍受着痛苦，每隔一小时就服一片止痛药。

---

cheek *n.* 脸颊

unbearable *adj.* 不能忍受的；令人不能容忍的

swollen *adj.* 肿胀的

painkiller *n.* 镇痛剂；止痛药

However, the tooth hurt so much when he tried to eat lunch that he knew he had to go to the dentist.

He asked his boss for time off. His boss could see that James was in great pain, and told him to take the rest of the day off.

The dentist agreed to see James immediately.

"Open your mouth," he said, "and let's have a look."

James opened his mouth.

"Which tooth is giving you trouble?" the dentist asked next.

James touched the tooth with his finger.

The dentist *x-rayed* the tooth, and then he put the x-ray against a bright light.

然而，吃中午饭时，他疼得受不了了，不得不去看牙医。

他向老板请假，老板看出詹姆斯忍受着极大的痛苦，于是同意他后半天可以不用工作。

牙医也同意立即给詹姆斯看病。

"张开嘴让我看看，"牙医说。

詹姆斯张开嘴。

"哪只牙疼？"牙医接着问。

詹姆斯用手指碰碰那颗牙。

牙医照了X光，并把X光片对着灯光看。

X-ray *v.* 给……拍X光片   cavity *n.* 蛀洞

"Oh, yes," he said, "I can see the problem. There is a *cavity* in the tooth. I'm afraid the hole is too big to fill. I'll have to take the tooth out."

"That's all right," James said. "Just stop the pain."

The dentist gave James an *injection* and quickly pulled out the tooth. He dropped it into the *garbage can*.

"Don't throw it away," James said. "Let me have it please."

"Why do you want your old tooth?" the dentist asked.

"I'm going to take it home, put it in a bowl of hot *honey* and watch it *suffer*," James said.

"噢，是的，"他说："我看出问题了。这颗牙上有个洞，恐怕洞太大了无法填充，拔掉吧。"

"好吧，"詹姆斯答道，"只要能止痛就行。"

牙医给詹姆斯打了一针，迅速拔掉了那颗牙，扔进了垃圾筒。

"别扔！"詹姆斯说："给我吧！"

"为什么要颗烂牙呀？"牙医问。

"我把它带回家，放在热蜂蜜水里，看着它痛苦！"詹姆斯说。

---

injection *n.* （向体内）注射（液体，尤指药液）　　garbage can 垃圾箱

honey *n.* 蜂蜜　　　　　　　　　　　　　　　　suffer *v.* 遭受；经受

The Last Laugh

Terry Wiltshire was a truck driver. He drove a huge truck from one end of the country to the other and ate most of his meals in *roadside* cafés.

On one occasion he drove up to a café and parked his truck. Then he went inside and ordered a meal. A waitress took it to his table.

笑到最后

特里·威尔特郡是一名卡车司机，他开着大型卡车穿越全国各地，大部分时间都在路边的餐馆吃饭。

一次，他在一家餐馆旁把车停了下来，然后进去点了饭菜，一名女侍者端来了他要的东西。

roadside *adj.* 路边的

Terry was eating his meal and minding his own business when three *bikers* came into the café. They were big, rough men who rode motorcycles. They wore *leather* and had *tattoos* on their arms.

The bikers saw Terry sitting alone at a table eating his meal. They decided to have some fun with him.

The biggest biker walked up to him and said, "Buy us a meal."

Terry shook his head. "I'm sorry. I don't buy meals for people I don't know."

"Then we'll soon make you know us," the leader of the bikers said, and pushed Terry.

Another of the bikers took Terry's food away from him and began eating it himself.

The third biker picked up Terry's cup of coffee and poured it all

---

特里正专心致志地用餐，三个骑摩托车的人进来了：他们高大、粗野，穿着皮衣皮裤，手臂上刺着文身。

三个人看到特里一个人用餐，便决定戏弄他。

最高大的一个骑手走向特里，并说："请我们吃这顿饭。"

特里摇摇头说："对不起，我从不请陌生人吃饭。"

"那我们就认识一下，"三个人中的老大说，并用手推搡特里。

另一个人则把特里的饭端走，并吃了起来。

第三个人拿起特里的咖啡，把咖啡倒在了特里的头上。

---

biker *n.* 骑自行车或摩托车的人　　　　　　　　　　leather *n.* 皮革
tattoo *n.* 文身

over Terry's head.

All this time, Terry said nothing. He did not even move. He sat quite still and let the bikers do what they liked.

When they were bored with their "fun", they walked away from him to another table. Then Terry stood up, left the café and drove away in his truck.

A waitress went to the bikers' table to get their order.

"Did you see that man?" the leader of the bikers said. "What a *coward*! He just sat there while we pushed him around. He wasn't much of a man, was he?"

"No," the waitress said with a smile, "and he wasn't much of a driver either. He just drove his truck over three motorcycles."

从头到尾，特里一言不发，甚至动也没有动。他静静地坐着，任这三个骑车人为所欲为。

当他们厌烦了这种"把戏"后，便走开坐到了另一张桌子旁。特里站起身，离开了餐馆，开车走了。

一个女侍者来到了三个骑车人的桌旁，让他们点菜。

"看见那个人了吗？"三个人中的老大说："真是个懦夫！我们把他差来遣去，他都不敢动。真算不上一个男人！"

"的确，"侍者笑着说："他也算不上一个好司机，他刚刚开着卡车碾碎了三辆摩托车！"

---

coward *n.* 胆小鬼；懦夫

The Right Price

The Gordon family was spending a day on the beach.

Mr and Mrs Gordon were sitting on the sand, reading their magazines. Mr Gordon was too stingy to rent a chair. Their twelve-year old daughter Sandra, was playing at the water's *edge*.

Suddenly a huge *wave* lifted Sandra up and carried her out to sea.

合理的价格

戈登一家在海滨度假，戈登先生和太太正坐在沙滩上读杂志。戈登先生太吝啬了，连一把椅子也舍不得租。他们12岁的女儿，桑德拉，在海边嬉戏。

突然一个巨浪袭来，把桑德拉掀起抛入了海里。

edge *n.* 边；边缘   wave *n.* 波浪

Fortunately, a *lifeguard* was on duty and he saw the wave carry Sandra away.He ran along the beach and *dove* into the sea. He swam quickly to where the girl, with her head only just above the water, was shouting for help.

She was very frightened. When the lifeguard reached her, she *struggled* with him, as *drowning* people often do.

However, he knew what to do and soon took hold of her and swam with her back to the beach.

By the time he reached it, Mr and Mrs Gordon had realized what had happened. They had run down to the water's edge.

Neither of them could swim. They just stood in the shallow water

---

幸运的是，一个救生员正值班，看到巨浪卷走了桑德拉，便沿着海滨跑，跳进海里。他快速地游向女孩，此时女孩的头刚刚露出水面，正大声呼救。

女孩恐惧极了，当救生员摸着她时，她像所有溺水的人一样拼命地挣扎着。

但是，救生员知道怎么做，很快就抓住她朝海滩游去。

直到这时，戈登先生和太太才意识到发生了什么事，他们跑向水边。

可他俩都不会游泳，只能站在浅水处，替女儿担心。救生员能及时救出女儿吗？

---

lifeguard *n.* 救生员

struggle *v.* 挣扎；奋斗

dive *v.* 跳水

drown *v.* （使）溺死

and worried about their daughter. Had the lifeguard reached her in time?

Fortunately, he had.

"That was quick work, young man," Mr Gordon said. He turned to his wife. "Give the lifeguard a dollar."

"A dollar?" Sandra cried. "Dad, how can you give him a dollar? He saved my life! I was half dead!"

"Quite right girl," Mr Gordon said, pleased by his daughter's *awareness* of the *value* of money.

He turned to his wife again and said, "She's right. She was only half dead. Give him fifty cents."

幸运的是，他做到了。

"真是太神速了，年轻人，"戈登先生说，他转向太太，"给救生员1美元。"

"1美元？"桑德拉喊道："爸爸，你怎么能给人1美元呢？他救了我的命！我都快半死了！"

"太对了！孩子！"戈登先生说。他很高兴看到女儿对金钱的价值有了认识。

他又转向太太说："女儿说得对，她只不过是半死，给他50美分！"

---

awareness *n.* 意识；认识   value *n.* 价值

46

Welcome Stranger

It was a dark and windy night. The wind *howled* and the rain beat down.

Harry and his wife were in bed. Although Harry slept through the storm, his wife woke up. She lay in bed, unable to sleep, listening to the noise of the storm.

Suddenly she heard a different noise. It sounded like someone *tapping* on the window.

欢迎你，不速之客！

这是一个漆黑的狂风呼啸的夜晚，风怒吼着，雨倾盆而下。

哈里和妻子躺在床上。外面虽然暴风骤雨，哈里依然入睡了，可妻子却一直睡不着。她躺在床上，无法入眠，倾听着暴风雨的声音。

突然她听到了一种异样的声音，像是有人敲打着窗户。

howl *v.* 嚎叫；咆哮   tap *v.* 轻拍；轻敲

She was very frightened. She woke her husband up.

"Harry," she whispered, "there's someone outside. Listen."

"It's nothing," he said, "just a *branch* of a tree tapping against the window in the wind. Go back to sleep."

He turned over and went back to sleep.

The tapping continued. It got louder and louder, and then the window began to *rattle*.

Harry's wife woke him up again.

"Harry, it isn't just the wind. There's somebody there. I know there is. Get up and look."

Harry got out of bed and walked across the room to the window. He pulled the curtain a little and looked out. He saw a man standing

---

她非常害怕，于是推醒了丈夫。

"哈里！"她低声喊道："外面有人，听！"

"没事的，"他答道："树枝在风中抽打窗户而已，睡吧。"

他翻了个身又睡了。

敲击声继续着。声音越来越大，窗户也开始吱吱作响。

妻子又把他弄醒了。

"哈里，不只是风，是人，一定有人。快起来看看！"

哈里起来走到窗前，他把窗帘拉开，向外望去。他看到一个人站在窗

---

branch n. 树枝   rattle v. （使）发嘎嘎声；（使）碰撞声

on a *ladder* outside the window. He smiled at the man and then went back to bed.

"Well?" his wife asked. "Was there anyone there?"

"Yes," Harry said. "There's a *burglar* trying to get in."

"Then do something!" his wife cried. "Phone the police!"

"Not yet," Harry said. "Wait until he opens the window. I've been trying to get it open since we had the house painted last year."

外梯子上，他冲那人笑一笑，然后回到床上。

"嗯？"妻子问："有人吧？"

"是的，"哈里答道："有个夜贼正试图进来。"

"那赶紧报警啊！"妻子喊道。

"先不用，"哈里说："等他把窗户打开再说。自从去年我们把房间刷上油漆后，我就一直试图能把窗户打开。"

---

ladder *n.* 梯子

burglar *n.* 窃贼

The Sound of Speed

Kathy was a college student. Like most students she had very little money, but she wanted to buy a car.

"If I can buy a really cheap one that works," she thought, "I will save money on bus *fares*. Then I'll have more to spend on food."

She spent a day looking at cars in *used car yards*. Most of the cars

---

速度的声音

凯茜是名大学生，像大多数学生一样，她几乎没有什么钱，可她想买辆车。

"如果我买一辆非常便宜的车——能开就行的那种，就会省下车票钱。那样我就会有更多的钱买吃的。"她想。

她花一整天时间在二手车市场看车。大部分的车都太贵了，最后她终于发现了一辆只要250美元的车。

---

fare *n.* 车费
car yard 车市

used *adj.* 旧的；二手的

were much too expensive, but at last she found one for $250.

The car was *rusty* and the paint was badly damaged, but it worked.

"It's got a good *engine*," the salesman said, "and the *gearbox* is OK. Forget everything else."

Kathy bought the car and drove it out of the car yard. Everything was wrong with it except for the engine and gearbox, which worked very well. "As long as they work," Kathy thought, "nothing else matters. The salesman was right."

Unfortunately, a few days later, while she was driving to her university, a police car drove up beside her and made her stop. A young policeman got out of his car and walked around Kathy's car. He looked at it *disbelievingly*.

这辆车锈迹斑斑，漆也严重脱落了，但还能开。

"这车发动机非常好，"销售商说："变速器运转也不错，其他的不用考虑。"

凯茜买下了车，开出了车市。发动机和变速器运转良好，但其他的糟透了。"只要这两个部件能工作就行，其他的都不重要，销售商说得对。"凯茜想。

不幸的是，几天后，当她开车上学时，一辆警车追了过来，迫使她停车。一个年轻的警察走下车，绕着凯茜的车边走边用怀疑的眼神打量着这辆破车。

---

rusty *adj.* 锈的
gearbox *n.* 齿轮箱；变速箱

engine *n.* 引擎；发动机
disbelievingly *adv.* 怀疑地；不相信地

He made a list of the things wrong with the car. It was a very long list.

Then he looked inside the car.

"Does your *speedometer* work?" he asked.

Kathy shook her head. "It is against the law, Miss," he said, "not to know how fast you are traveling."

Kathy smiled at him sweetly.

"Oh, but I do know how fast I am traveling," she said. "Up to 30 *miles* an hour, the doors rattle. Between 31 and 50 miles an hour, the whole car rattles. Over 50 miles an hour, I rattle."

他列出了一长串车的毛病来。

然后他向车里看看，"你的速度表在运转吗？"他问。

凯茜摇摇头。

"小姐，不知道开车的速度是多少，这违反法律规定。"

凯茜冲他甜甜一笑。

"噢，可我知道我开得有多快。"她说："每小时达到30英里时，车门就吱吱发抖。每小时31英里到50英里之间时，整个车都吱吱发抖。每小时超过50英里时，我就吱吱发抖啦。"

---

speedometer *n.* （汽车等）速度计

mile *n.* 英里

48

The Cow

Henry was driving along a country road when his car began to behave badly. The engine stopped running *smoothly* and the car moved forward in *jerks*.

He drove along like this for several miles, and finally decided to stop and look at the engine. He did not know very much about engines, but he thought something might be broken.

牛

亨利正开着车沿着乡间小路行驶时，车出了问题。发动机转动不太平稳，车子向前一窜一窜地行驶。

就这样开了几英里后，他决定停车检查一下发动机。他对发动机知之甚少，但他肯定车一定出了什么故障。

---

smoothly *adv.* 顺利地；没有问题地   jerk *n.* 猛拉；猛地一动

He stopped the car, but did not turn off the engine, and got out. Then he lifted the *hood* and looked inside. He could not see anything wrong, but the engine was still not running smoothly.

Then he heard a voice say, "It's probably the *fuel pump*."

Henry stood up, and looked around. Except for a dark brown cow with a white circle on its nose in a nearby field, there was no one around.

Frightened by the voice, Henry quickly closed the hood, got into the car and drove off.

He soon came to a small *gas station*. He drove in and parked, and after a few moments an old man came up to him.

"What's the problem?" he asked Henry.

他停下车，没有关闭发动机就跳了下去。他掀开引擎盖，向里看，没看出什么毛病来。可发动机仍然运转不自如。

然后他听到一个声音说：“可能是供油泵出了问题。”

亨利站起来，向四周望去。四周空无一人，附近田地里有一头黄牛站在那里，鼻子上有个白圈。

他被这个声音吓坏了，迅速关上引擎盖，跳进车里开走了。

很快他来到了一个小加油站，他把车子开进去，停下来。过一会儿，一个老人走了过来。

“怎么了？”他问亨利。

---

hood *n.* 引擎罩
gas station 加油站

fuel pump 油泵

"The engine's not running smoothly," Henry said.

The old man lifted up the hood and looked inside. Then he unscrewed one of the *spark plugs*, looked at it, cleaned it and screwed it back in place.

"You had a dirty spark plug," he said. "She'll be all right now."

"I heard a voice tell me it was probably the fuel pump," Henry said to the old man. "But when I looked around, I couldn't see anyone."

The old man smiled. "Except a brown cow with a white circle on its nose?"

"Yes, that's right."

"You don't want to pay any attention to her," the old man said. "She doesn't know anything about cars."

"发动机运转不正常，"亨利回答。

老人掀开引擎盖，向里看看。他拧开其中一个火花塞，看了一下，又清洗干净，然后拧紧。

"火花塞脏了"，他说："现在没问题了"。

"我听到一个声音告诉我可能是供油泵有问题，"亨利告诉老人："但当我向四周看时，却什么人也没看到。"

老人笑了，说："除了一头鼻子上带白圈的黄牛？"

"是的，太对了。"

"别理她，"老人说，"她对车一点儿也不了解。"

---

spark plug 火花塞

49

Aunt Ethel

One day, Jenny and Simon Lang received a letter.

"Dear Jenny and Simon," the letter said. "I have decided to spend the rest of my life visiting my *nephews* and *nieces*. I plan to stay with each of you in turn. I am looking forward to visiting you very soon. I will, of course, remember your kindness

埃塞尔姑妈

一天，詹妮和西蒙收到了一封信。

"亲爱的詹妮和西蒙，"信中说，"我已经决定，余生将和侄子和侄女们一起度过，我计划和你们轮流过。盼望很快见到你们。当然，在遗嘱中我会记得你们的善良和慷慨大度。你们知道，我过世的丈夫挣了很多钱，我非常富有。爱你们的埃塞尔姑妈。"

---

nephew *n.* 侄子；外甥　　　　　　　　niece *n.* 侄女；外甥女

and *generosity* in my *will*. As you know, my late husband made a lot of money and I am a wealthy woman. Love, Aunt Ethel."

Jenny and Simon had not been married very long and they were poor. "We must make the old woman welcome," Simon said. "Then she'll leave us a lot of money."

"I agree," Jenny said. "Let's hope she's really old, so she'll die soon."

"Yes, and let's hope she dies while she's with us. Then we'll get most of her money."

When Aunt Ethel arrived, Jenny and Simon made her feel very welcome. They gave her the best room in the house for her bedroom, and cooked delicious meals for her.

Unfortunately, Aunt Ethel was not easy to please. In fact, she

---

詹妮和西蒙结婚不久，非常穷。"我们一定要让老人高兴，"西蒙说："这样她就能留给我们一大笔钱。"

"我同意，"詹妮说："但愿她年纪非常大了，那样很快就会死的。"

"是啊，让我们祈愿她和我们一同住时死去，那样我们就能得到大部分钱。"

当埃塞尔姑妈来时，詹妮和西蒙把她照顾得非常好，把最好的房间让给她做卧房，为她煮最美味的食物。

不幸的是，埃塞尔姑妈很难被取悦。事实上，她是个可怜的、坏脾气

---

generosity *n.* 慷慨；大方

will *n.* 遗嘱

was a miserable, *bad-tempered*, *selfish* woman. She made Jenny and Simon very unhappy. Everything they did was wrong, and she was always complaining.

"I don't know how long I can live like this," Jenny said one day. "I'm working like a *slave* for that old woman. I cook her food, wash her clothes, mend her clothes, clean her room, and do her shopping for her. I have no time for myself at all."

"Be patient," Simon said. "She's old. She'll die soon."

But the years passed, and it looked as if Aunt Ethel was never going to die. Jenny often *quarreled* with Simon. Aunt Ethel had destroyed their happiness.

的、自私自利的老妇人。这让詹妮和西蒙都很不愉快。他俩做的一切都是错的，她总在不停地抱怨。

"不知道这样下去还能坚持多久，"一天，詹妮说："我像个奴隶一样伺候她：给她煮饭、洗衣服、补衣服、打扫房间、买东西。我自己一点儿时间也没有了。"

"耐心点儿，"西蒙说，"她老了，很快就会死了。"

但一年一年过去了，埃塞尔姑妈似乎永远不会死去。詹妮常常与西蒙吵架，埃塞尔姑妈破坏了他们的幸福。

---

bad-tempered *adj.* 坏脾气的
slave *n.* 奴隶

selfish *adj.* 自私的
quarrel *v.* 争吵；吵架

Then suddenly, one day Aunt Ethel died. Jenny and Simon were very happy. They were free at last.

"I couldn't have lived with your aunt in this house much longer," Jenny said.

"What do you mean, my aunt?" Simon said. "I thought she was your aunt."

一天，埃塞尔姑妈突然死了。詹妮和西蒙高兴极了，他们终于自由了。

"我再也无法与你姑妈在这个房子里一起住下去了。"詹妮说。

"什么叫'我'的姑妈？"西蒙回答说："我一直以为她是'你'的姑妈。"

Famous Last Words

When someone who is in good health dies suddenly, there is usually an *inquest*.

An inquest is a kind of *court* of inquiry. The person in charge of an inquest is called a *coroner*. His job is to find out exactly how a person died.

If there is nothing *suspicious* about the death, he will decide that the person died from natural causes

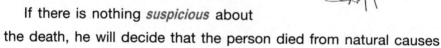

经典的遗言

当某个身体健康的人突然死亡时，常常要验尸。

验尸是一种司法审讯程序，负责讯问的人被称为验尸官。他的工作是查找一个人真正的死因。

如果死亡没有任何可疑之处，他就会裁决此人属于正常死亡或死于意外事故。但如果他觉得可疑，就会裁决此人为非正常死亡，即可能是他杀。

inquest *n.* 审讯；验尸
coroner *n.* 验尸官

court *n.* 法庭，法院
suspicious *adj.* 可疑的

or an accident. If, however, he is suspicious, he may decide that the person's death was caused by a person or persons unknown.

At one inquest, the coroner was trying to find out exactly what had caused the death of a local businessman, Henry Watson.

The man's *widow* was giving her *evidence*. She was very *upset* and had to stop from time to time. The coroner did not want to upset her more than necessary, but he had to find out the truth. There were questions he had to ask.

"Mrs Watson, I know this is painful for you," he said, "but I want you to think very carefully and then answer my questions. You and your husband were having dinner at home. Is that correct?"

"Yes."

"Suddenly he fell to the floor?"

"Yes."

在一次验尸中，验尸官试图查明当地一个商人——亨利·沃森的死因。

他的遗孀正在提供证词。她情绪极度不稳定，不得不时常停下来。验尸官不想给她带来不必要的烦恼，但他必须查明真相，有些问题他不得不问。

"沃森夫人，我知道这会令你很痛苦，"他说，"但我仍想让您仔细考虑好了再作答。您和您的丈夫当时在家里共进晚餐，是这样吗？"

"是的。"

"突然他就倒在了地上？"

"是的。"

---

widow *n.* 寡妇；遗孀　　　　　　　　　　evidence *n.* 证词，证据
upset *adj.* 心烦意乱的；担忧的

"You stood up and hurried to him? You *knelt* beside him? He was in great pain?"

"Yes."

"Did he say anything?"

The widow lowered her head.

"Please, Mrs Watson, you must answer the question. What were his last words?"

The widow took a deep breath and then spoke. "He said," she whispered, "'I'm not surprised you were charged only 50 cents for that seafood we had for dinner.'"

"你站起来冲了过去？跪在他旁边？他极度痛苦？"

"是的。"

"他说什么了没有？"

这个寡妇低下了头。

"沃森夫人，您必须回答这个问题。他的遗言是什么？"

这个寡妇深深吸了一口气，然后说："他说……"她几乎是低语道，"我一点儿也不惊讶，你只用50美分买下了我们晚餐吃的海鲜。"

---

kneel *v.* 屈膝；下跪

The Longest Menu in the World

man walked into a restaurant that advertised having the longest menu in the world. The manager was very *proud* of being able to provide any dish, no matter how unusual.

At the bottom of the menu, there was a notice that said, "If you do not see the dish you require on this menu, please tell us and we will add it to the menu immediately."

世界上最长的菜单

一个人走进一家打着"拥有世界上最长菜单"广告的餐馆。不论多么特别的菜肴,本餐馆都能提供,经理为此感到特别自豪。

菜单的最下面写着一则小启事: "如果您在本菜单上没找到您需要的菜肴,请告诉我们。我们会立即把它添加到菜单上。"

---

proud *adj.* 自豪的;引以为荣的

One day a man walked in, looked at the menu and decided to make life really difficult for the manager and his *chef*. He would order something that was very unusual.

When the waiter came up to take his order, he said, "You say you can serve any dish, anything at all, even if it's not on your menu, which is the longest menu in the world."

"That is correct, sir. We have never yet been unable to meet our customers' requirements."

"Very well," the man said. "In that case, bring me two elephant ears on *toast*. Indian, not African."

The waiter wrote down on his pad: Two Indian elephant ears on toast.

一天，一个人走进这家餐馆，看到了这份菜单，便决定给经理和厨师出一道难题。他想点一些特别的东西。

服务生过来问他要点什么菜，他说："你们说能提供任何一种菜肴，任何一种，哪怕是你们这份世界上最长的菜单上没有的菜？"

"是的，先生。我们向来都能满足顾客的任何需要。"

"很好，"他说，"这样的话，我要两片配有烤面包片的象耳，要印度象耳，不要非洲象耳。"

服务生在小单上记下了"两片配有烤面包片的印度象耳"。

---

chef *n.* 厨师；主厨

toast *n.* 烤面包片

"Very good, sir," he said. "That shouldn't take long."

He walked quickly away.

The man was very surprised and rather disappointed.

Then he smiled as the waiter returned with a very unhappy look on his face.

"Ah!" the man said. "You can't bring me elephant ears on toast, can you?"

The waiter was very *apologetic*.

"I'm very sorry sir, and this is most *embarrassing*," he said, "but I'm afraid we can't. Unfortunately, we're run out of bread."

"非常好，"他说，"应该不会需要太长时间的。"

说完很快地走了。

这个人非常惊讶并且相当地失望。

看到服务生很不开心地回来，他马上就微笑起来。

"哈！"他说，"你们一定是没法给我上这道菜吧！"

服务生非常抱歉地说："对不起，先生，这实在是最令人尴尬的一件事，恐怕我们真的没法给您上这道菜了。很不幸，我们的面包已经售完了。"

---

apologetic *adj.* 道歉的；抱歉的　　　embarrassing *adj.* 令人窘迫的；令人为难的

Court Case

Jack Evans quarreled with his neighbor, Ellen Brown. Mrs Brown had a dog. Jack did not like dogs. He wanted Mrs Brown to give away or sell her dog, but she *refused*.

"I'll take you to *court* if you don't," he said.

Mrs Brown laughed at him. She was not worried.

Jack thought, "I must talk to a *lawyer*, but lawyers are expensive.

法庭诉讼

杰克·埃文斯和邻居艾伦·布朗吵了一架。布朗太太有一条狗，可杰克不喜欢狗。他希望布朗太太把狗送走或是卖了，但她拒绝这么做。

"如果您不答应的话，我会把您告上法庭。"杰克说。

布朗太太对此付之一笑，她并不为此担心。

杰克想："我必须找个律师谈谈，可律师费太贵了。我可不想浪费自己的钱。如果这场官司不能取胜，那就浪费钱了。"

---

refuse *v.* 拒绝；回绝   court *n.* 法院
lawyer *n.* 律师

I don't want to waste my money. I will waste it if I don't win my *case* against Mrs Brown and her dog."

Then Jack had an idea. There was a young lawyer in the town. He did not have much work. Not many people knew about him. "I'll visit him," Jack thought. "He needs work."

He visited the young lawyer in his office. "I need some advice," he said.

"Certainly," the young lawyer said. "What is your problem? I am here to help you."

"Good. I want to take my neighbor to court. However, I will pay for your advice only if you think I will win the case in court."

The lawyer was not pleased by this suggestion. However, he had very little work. Here was a chance to get some.

最后他想出了个好办法。城里有一个年轻的律师，业务不多，知道他的人也不太多。"我去找他，"杰克想，"他需要业务。"

杰克来到事务所找到这位年轻的律师。"我想咨询一些问题。"他说。

"当然可以，"年轻的律师说，"您遇到什么麻烦了？我会帮助您的。"

"好。我想把邻居告上法庭。但是，除非您有取胜的把握，我才会付律师费。"

听了这话，律师不太高兴。但是，他的业务实在太少了，这正是个好机会。

---

case *n.* 诉讼；官司

"All right," he said. "I agree. I will listen to your problem. I will give you honest advice. You will pay me only if I think you can win in court."

Jack told him about the problem. The lawyer listened carefully. Sometimes he made notes. When Jack finished, the lawyer sat back in his chair and said, "You will win your case. I have no doubt about it. May I take your case to court?"

Jack stood up and walked towards the door. "No, thank you," he said. "I will not take it to court."

"What about my *fee*?" the lawyer asked. "You have to keep your promise."

"I am keeping my *promise*," Jack said. "I will not win in court. You see, I did not tell you my case, I told you Mrs Brown's."

"好吧，"他说，"我同意。把您的问题说给我听听，我会真诚地给您建议。如果我认定您能赢这场官司，您再付钱。"

杰克便把事情的原委告诉了他。律师听得非常认真，有时还记记笔记。律师听完后，往后倚在椅背上说，"您一定会赢的，毫无疑问。需要我把这案子提交到法庭上吗？"

杰克站了起来，向门口走去，说："不，谢谢您了。我不准备上法庭。"

"那我的咨询费呢？"律师问道，"您必须要履行自己的诺言。"

"我在履行自己的诺言呀。"杰克说，"我不会赢这场官司的。您看，我刚才说的不是我的情况，而是布朗太太的。"

---

fee *n.* 费用；酬金

promise *n.* 许诺；诺言